— To

Rev. Jack Hayford

When troubles cross your path, keep running
...with God at your side.

As Craig Larson notes, the trials and tribulations of life can sometimes seem like an endurance test. "In such situations we feel like runners in a long, dark night, unwilling entries in a midnight marathon. We can't see where we're going, yet somehow we must finish the race. We keep putting one foot in front of the other, all the while feeling as if our heart will burst and our legs collapse. Where is the dawn? Where is the finish line? *Is* there a finish line?"

In these pages, you'll learn that *Running the Midnight Marathon* can make you spiritually stronger. Discover the prizes you will earn by slowly trotting in faithful perseverance, knowing that God will guide and uphold you every step of the way.

May the Lord grant you great endurance to glorify Christ! Colossians 1:11

Craig Brian Larson

RUNNING
THE
MIDNIGHT MARATHON
CRAIG BRIAN LARSON

Fleming H. Revell Company
Tarrytown, New York

Unless otherwise identified, all Scripture quotations in this book are from the Holy Bible, New International Version, copyright © 1973, 1978, 1984 International Bible Society. Used by permission of Zondervan Bible Publishers.

Scripture verses identified KJV are from the King James Version of the Bible.

Scripture quotation in this publication identified NKJV is from The New King James Version. Copyright © 1979, 1980, 1982, Thomas Nelson, Inc., Publishers.

Scripture quotations identified NAS are from the New American Standard Bible, © The Lockman Foundation 1960, 1971, 1972, 1973, 1975, 1977.

Scripture quotation from The Amplified New Testament is copyright © The Lockman Foundation 1954, 1958, 1987.

Library of Congress Cataloging-in-Publication Data

Larson, Craig Brian.
    Running the midnight marathon / Craig Brian Larson.
        p.   cm.
    ISBN 0-8007-5394-1
    1. Christian life—1960– 2. Perseverance (Ethics) I. Title.
BV4501.2.L3345   1991
248.4—dc20   90-21923
                                                                  CIP

Copyright © 1991 by Craig Brian Larson
Published by the Fleming H. Revell Company
Tarrytown, New York 10591
Printed in the United States of America

For Christ and His kingdom.
Remembering my mom, Donna W. Larson.

Contents

RUNNING

THE

MIDNIGHT

MARATHON

1
Why Go On?

Aching words . . . sometimes thundering with anger . . . other times mild, emotions long ago spent, like a soft rain after a tornado: "Why go on? Why keep trying? Nothing good is coming out of this. I pray; I work; I try to do what's right, but nothing happens. I try to believe God's promises, but nothing changes."

On the horizon, more dark clouds and relentless, cold drizzle. "It seems like my life is being wasted. How can this be God's will? I can't go on like this."

These words express the feelings of many: The man whose sickness festers. The woman whose marriage is a combat zone. The Christian leader whose ministry crawls and sputters. An ache in the gut, a feeling of frustration, despair, and abandonment, gnaws at the student who toils at homework only to score a C minus on tests, or the mother who reads everything in the bookstore on child raising but whose teenager rebels, or the single parent who slaves at two jobs and still faces floggings from bills three months overdue.

Then there are the wars within. The nagging urge to quit, to escape, to get a new address in life also haunts those who have wrestled with life-controlling habits, and the emotionally troubled, who are trapped by depression, fear, loneliness, guilt, anxiety. Would it be accurate to say that the majority of us voice those aching words, if not often, at least occasionally?

In such situations we feel like runners in a long, dark night, unwilling entries in a midnight marathon. We can't see where we're going, yet somehow we must finish the race. We keep putting one foot in front of the other, all the while feeling as if our heart will burst and our legs collapse. Where is the dawn? Where is the finish line? Is there a finish line?

Any thinking person asks a logical question: Why persevere? We have every reason—a hundred logical reasons rehearsed over and over—to quit. Without some justification, why go on in a fruitless, extraordinarily difficult, seemingly impossible situation? Why continue to trust God to work for good?

Vince and Teri Chodor have asked questions. On July 26, 1984, Teri gave birth to their second child, a girl, whom they named Rebekah. The delivery had gone beautifully, and Rebekah appeared to be in perfect condition, rating a ten on the APGAR scale.

Rebekah moved into her cheerful nursery. As the weeks passed she continued healthy, except for some discoloration in her skin thought to be jaundice. At her six-week checkup, however, the doctor, noticing a blue tint to her lips, became immediately alarmed. He listened to her heart, then ordered that she be rushed to a specialist.

To Teri's bewilderment, a simple trip to the doctor's office quickly turned major medical. After an ambulance ride to Children's Memorial Hospital in Chicago, her baby underwent a heart-catheterization procedure, which involved inserting a tube into a leg vein and up into her heart. The terrifying diagnosis: Rebekah was in heart failure. She had only days to live.

"Her heart," said the cardiologist, "is a mess." The four pulmonary veins that pipe clean, oxygenated blood from the lungs to the heart were detached, dangling behind her heart, so that blood was being diverted to the liver. There were two holes in her heart allowing "clean" and "dirty" blood to mix. Also, instead of left and right ventricular outlets, she had two right outlets and no left. More revealing than the surgical report was the cardiologist's grim face.

"We were devastated," says Teri. "We fell on our faces to pray. All I could say was, 'Jesus, help!' For six weeks I had nursed and bathed and played with her. She even slept in our bed. I loved her so much. Now they were implying that she would die. I was so afraid I could hardly breathe."

Open-heart surgery was scheduled. The doctors planned to do just enough to keep her alive: to attach those four dangling pulmonary veins. Her other defects would have to wait until she was stronger. Two "this can't be happening to us" days after bringing their "healthy" baby to the pediatrician, Vince and Teri kissed her tenderly and watched as she was wheeled into OR.

The struggle was waged in two rooms. For six hours the surgeons worked with Rebekah. In the waiting room Vince and Teri prayed, read the Bible, and sang worship choruses with friends who had brought a guitar. Occasionally they were interrupted by a nurse bringing status reports from the operating room. She was guarded yet optimistic.

Finally she brought the biggest update. The crucial point of the surgery—when they would take Rebekah off the heart-lung machine and try to jolt her heart back into beating—had been accomplished with ease. To the astonishment of the doctors, Rebekah had bounded over her first high hurdle.

Those six hours had been long, but the next two weeks lasted forever. "The recovery involved constant monitoring," says Vince. "She could have died at any second. My wife lived at her bedside. Rebekah couldn't eat for three days. She couldn't drink for three days. We watched tears pour down her face. After a day's worth of crying, all we saw were the tears and her mouth open but silent; her voice was gone. So it was horrible. It was just horrible."

Nevertheless, she made it. With grateful hearts, after two weeks they brought Rebekah home. They had been tested to the limit. The ordeal, however, was just beginning, a year that Vince now describes as "a roller coaster."

Stress Points

Vince and Teri felt it—excruciating stress at three pressure points—and so will everyone who is struggling to persevere.

Physical

Long journeys pose particular problems. First, they're exhausting. Second, after embarking it can be impossible to refuel. With perseverance demanding heroic effort and energy, what do we do when we're pooped, when we feel like an ocean freighter with no more coal for the furnace, no more steam in the engine, no more churn in the props? Everything depends on our reaching our destination, but we're floating dead in the water.

As if that isn't bad enough, exhaustion can pull the plug elsewhere. It scrambles emotions and weakens willpower; as someone has said, "Fatigue makes cowards of us all."

Emotional

Feelings can be as unruly as ocean waves. "Sometimes I would have anxiety attacks at home," says Teri. "Suddenly this fear would grip me, and I couldn't breathe. Satan would put pictures in my mind of little caskets, a funeral, an empty crib. He put horrible things in my mind, constantly showing Rebekah to me dead. After about three seconds I would rebuke those thoughts. Sometimes it would last longer, though, because I let that fear grip me. Then I would start crying and panicking."

Not long ago I watched a newsclip of a town being flooded. The residents, forewarned that the nearby river would overflow, had sandbagged around homes, alongside streets, and at the riverbank. Nevertheless, the torrent overwhelmed them. Through windows and sewerage systems, muddy water was pouring into basements. Although homeowners mopped and bailed and sump pumps labored, they were fighting a losing battle.

The same scenario sometimes holds when we fight muddy emotions. As our ordeal wears on day after day, the murky waters of depression, fear, doubt, and anxiety seem irresistible. Sometimes, weary of the struggle, we just give in.

Spiritual

Trials inevitably test and quiz our faith. Questions arise, some posed by Satan, others from ourselves: "If God loves you, why hasn't He done something? If God is all-powerful, why is this happening? What good does prayer do?" Compounding our troubles, failed quizzes keep coming back.

If we permit doubts to prevail, a sense of insecurity—even terror—grips us; everything we have believed in and hoped for is giving way. A ship anchored in the harbor can weather a tempest, but, anchor broken away, the open seas beat and toss it unhindered.

For a few unsettling hours, Vince faced that possibility. "Okay, God, she might live," he reasoned, "and if she lives through all this, what a miracle! I'll praise You so much. But why do I have to go through all this? Things aren't making sense here. And then there's a chance she'll die, and if she dies, it's going to be horrible and traumatic, and everybody's lives will be changed forever. Why are You letting this happen? Why should she die?" Vince's anchor, nevertheless, held firm.

Somehow, despite the pain at these three stressful points, good things can happen.

One Priceless Lesson

Suffering for years myself at the same stress points, I learned one priceless lesson about perseverance. In June of 1979, I became pastor of a small church in the inner city of Chicago. Twenty-five of us met on Sunday mornings in a leaky, crumbling, seventy-five-year-old building. The weekly offerings averaged three hundred dollars, from which we payed expenses and my full-time salary. We suffered none of the temptations of prosperity.

For my first year, that salary added up to thirteen thousand dollars, which, to put it mildly, cramped our life-style. For four years we drove an old Malibu in which, when it rained, three to four inches of water would collect on the floor. For five years we lived in a second-floor apartment that was a drafty, uninsulated icebox in the winter and a sweltering oven in the summer: our two-bedroom appliance in the sky. A factory several blocks away treated children's clothes with formaldehyde to fireproof them. According to the EPA the smoke from their chimney was safe, but the odor, astringent and overwhelming, was deadly.

Unnerving things happened all too often. One Sunday night my wife had to stay home from church with the kids. Just after the service ended she telephoned. "Brian, something's happening downstairs. Hurry home."

Minutes later I found police cars parked in front of our apartment. Blood was splattered over the stairs and porch. "I live upstairs," I told the officers at the doorway.

"Don't worry," they said. "Everything's okay up there."

"What happened?"

"The two brothers got in a fight, and one of them grabbed a knife."

Thank God, although their kitchen was a sea of blood, no one died.

Other things contributed to lingering insecurity. Our landlord, who did not speak English, jury-rigged a basement apartment. Oblivious to technicalities like building codes and permits, he began blowing fuses. From then on whenever we went downstairs to do laundry, we would find screwdrivers left in the sockets.

And then there was the oversized challenge of developing a productive church. It felt like carving a statue from granite with your fingernails. The neighborhood seethed with the typical ills that disease the city and fill the headlines.

Sometimes I wavered. There were despairing times when I wanted to resign, but the Lord kept us in place. Although I was sometimes a pillar of steadfast determination, I often just held on, at times unwillingly, occasionally by the tips of my fingers. Because we didn't quit, however, God did something.

Brick by brick, living stone by living stone, He built His church. Progress was maddeningly slow as only a few people came to Christ yearly. But attendance did inch upward: approximately forty in 1982, seventy in 1984, ninety in 1986. We started ministries such as a food pantry, clubs for boys and girls, and neighborhood outreaches. Most important, the mortar of love was in ample supply.

In 1987, God directed me to resign. I felt deep satisfaction as I appraised our time there. The church was relatively small but established, with the mortgage paid off, a parsonage, committed leaders at their posts, solid income, and five thousand dollars in savings. By God's grace the church had progressed over eight and a half years, not spectacularly but steadily. Although the toll on me and my family had been steep, emotionally, physically, and financially, at the end we could say, "It was well worth it." In fact it broke our hearts to leave.

Through all of this, the Lord taught me a lesson I will never forget: Time is on my side. Although I am nothing special, if I simply persevere, with prayer and obedience, faith and work, the Lord will fulfill His perfect, better-than-I-could-ever-plan will for my life. With God as my friend, time is my ally.

My schooling, nevertheless, was incomplete.

One Anchoring Scripture

I certainly didn't think I needed to learn any more about perseverance, and I didn't expect to need much in our new church. Granted, it was struggling to survive—forty people attended on Sunday mornings, and the weekly offerings fell four hundred dollars short of break-even—but I thought we would progress quickly. Wrong, wrong, naively wrong.

The first six months (without going into details) were excruciating. In addition we still felt a painful loss over our previous church. In many respects, it seemed we had lost everything. Yet I knew God had led us; never had any decision been confirmed to me in so many ways.

During this period of grief, a sanity-saving Scripture, Hebrews 10:36, caught my attention:

> You need to persevere
> so that when you have done the will of God,
> you will receive what he has promised.

Prior to this I had never sensed the weight of this verse, but now it became my anchor. I memorized it and in times of despair would repeat it over and over and over. It taught me two lessons:

1. *There is usually a delay between our obedience to God's will and the fulfillment of His promise.* Often we step out to follow God based on an assumption that is quite different. Subconsciously we expect that when we obey God, everything should go well, that obedience is like rubbing a rabbit's foot. Rough times disorient us. "What's going on, Lord?" we wonder. "I'm obeying. Why aren't You holding up Your end of the agreement?" Through Hebrews 10:36, however, I realized I was in the hiatal pause of promise.

2. *By giving up, I would forfeit what God had promised.* This verse showed me the cost of quitting. If I folded tent, the pain already suffered would be wasted and future blessings lost.

Despite the anguish, I had to obey longer than a while; rather, I had to persevere as long as necessary.

God's promised blessings can be nipped in the bud. For their fulfillment resembles the blooming of a rose. The bud forms, hard and small and green, nothing particularly attractive. Yet, bound tightly inside are the forming petals, soft and red and delicate. The petals grow unseen. Only later as the rose blooms do we see their beauty. So it is with God's work. His perfect plans for us are forming in the bud—secretly—and as we persevere, we will, in God's perfect time, see them blossom. Philippians 2:13 promises, "It is God who works in you to will and to act according to his good purpose."

That good purpose is the subject of the coming ten chapters. We will examine the rosebud. And we will find ten gorgeous reasons to persevere.

2
To Realize God's Promise

When running the midnight marathon, a few momentous words from God can mean the difference between hope and despair, strength and weakness—even life and death.

Rebekah's frail body was deathly weak when I went to visit her prior to her first surgery. After donning a sterile yellow gown and scrubbing my hands with a plastic brush and brown, disinfectant soap, I pressed with Vince into the thick tension of the intensive care unit of Children's Memorial Hospital in Chicago. We passed a row of sick babies, each in a clear-plastic, saucerlike bed.

I greeted Teri, whose face was taut with strain, and then turned my attention to Rebekah. She lay unconscious, her eyes moist and swollen. She was wrapped, not in pink baby blankets, but technology. Two feet overhead a lamp radiated heat. A welter of wires and tubes networked her tiny body, and around the saucer-bed stood monitors and IVs and shelves filled with emergency supplies. On the electronic screen, I observed the slow-fluttering record of her heartbeat, now in such jeopardy.

Then I noticed something with a human touch. Taped

above Rebekah's head was a handwritten note. "My flesh and my heart may fail," it said, "but God is the strength of my heart and my portion forever. Psalm 73:26." Amidst such fragility, these words—with the divine touch—stood like bedrock. Calm. Strong. Eternal.

They had met an immediate need. "While I was in bed last night," Teri told me, "I prayed, 'God, You have to tell me, is she going to die? Is she going to live? I can't stand this. I'm just so afraid because I don't know.' Then I opened the Bible and found that Scripture. My eyes fell right to it. I said, 'O God, I know that's what You're telling me. And I'm going to trust You.' So I wrote it out, ran to ICU, and taped it to her bed. Then I went back to the quiet room and slept like a log."

A few momentous words from God. I sensed Teri was clinging as tightly to that Scripture as she had held Rebekah the day before. Over the coming months, with their dizzying emotional swings, Vince and Teri continued to squeeze that promise like the handrail on a roller coaster.

It made endurance possible. Psalm 73:26 gave Vince and Teri a logical reason to persevere. God's promises do the same for anyone. We persevere in order to see them fulfilled.

Albeit logical, it's not easy. Another human, unspiritual logic argues stubbornly against God's words. Many, nevertheless, overcome. I have observed that those who enduringly squeeze the stainless steel handrail of promise understand four crucial ideas.

God Generally Follows a Modus Operandi

God is somewhat predictable. That is to say, His dealings with people as recorded in the Bible follow a certain pattern. He promises, then waits—sometimes long, sometimes not so long—to see whether we respond properly, with faith, and finally He fulfills His words. Thus, we can identify three stages: promise, delay, and fulfillment.

We prefer but one stage: miracle. *Why the delay?* we wonder. *Why must I wait?* Whatever the reason, it isn't as if God were slighting us. He followed this time-intensive pattern with one of the Bible's greatest men. "God made his promise to Abraham . . . saying, 'I will surely bless you and give you many descendants.' And so *after waiting patiently*, Abraham received what was promised" (Hebrews 6:13–15 italics added).

Patiently indeed. Twenty-five years Abraham waited for Isaac, who was promised when Abraham was seventy-five and born when he was one hundred. The fact is, by human standards God is slow.

Disillusionment seeps in when we forget the time frame over which the Lord performed miracles in the Bible. He is the God of mighty deeds, yet many of His mightiest deeds followed a protracted wait. Israel's exodus out of Egypt, the event celebrated thereafter as the prototype act of God on behalf of His people, occurred 430 years after Jacob migrated there. From the first prophecy of a Messiah until the actual birth of Christ, thousands of years passed. Little wonder that 2 Peter 3:8 says, "With the Lord . . . a thousand years are like a day."

Long time frames also come into play for notable individuals. At age seventeen Joseph, great-grandson of Abraham, learned through a divinely inspired dream that he would someday hold sway as a ruler. In short order his own brothers brokered him into slavery. Worse yet, after several years as a favored house servant, he was falsely accused and then dumped into a dungeon. More years passed, as pencil marks on a prison wall. At long last he miraculously interpreted a dream for Pharaoh, won his favor, and became Egypt's chief administrator at age thirty. Thirteen torturous years after his prophetic dream.

Moses knew a little about extended waits. Plucked from the Nile by Pharaoh's daughter, he was raised silver-spoon style in the royal house. Yet, at age forty, remembering his Hebrew blood and sensing the call to deliver his people from bondage, Moses killed an Egyptian guard to rescue an Israelite. Then he fled from Pharaoh, ending up as a lowly shepherd on the back side of a desert. Decades drifted by like the dunes. Then he saw a burning bush . . . he talked with God . . . he went to deliver Israel out of bondage—at age eighty. Since his first rescue effort, forty dry years had passed.

David, too, discovered God's patience. When he was a teenager, Samuel the prophet anointed him Israel's next king (though the backslidden King Saul still reigned). Such divine appointment should, in our minds, mean clear sailing into the throne room, and the breezes did look favorable when he downed Goliath and later, as an army commander, scored triumph upon triumph. But Saul's response—jealousy and assassination attempts—precipitated a change of scenery for David, in fact several changes: a few years in the Judean wilderness, some time in alien Gath, feigning insanity, then to other foreign soil at Mizpah, and another year and a half with archenemy Philistines. Eventually King Saul fell in battle. David, now thirty years old, was acclaimed king—but of only one of the twelve tribes. Finally, after seven and a half years of civil war, the other eleven tribes also pledged allegiance. Since his selection by Samuel, at least seventeen turbulent years had transpired.

Apparently if you've had to linger awhile for the fulfillment of God's promise, you're in good company.

The Lord's method—promise, delay, fulfillment—hasn't changed. Nor has what is required of us. I have learned something from Abraham, and my wife, about that.

Promises Are Like Property

Those who cling tenaciously to God's promises view them from a unique perspective. Several years ago on our anniversary, my wife, Nancy, gave me a little handmade booklet. On the purple cover, it said something romantic like "For My Lover." Inside I found a dozen homespun coupons, redeemable for priceless favors such as "One hot batch of chocolate chip cookies," "A back rub for fifteen minutes," or "Your favorite dinner." She had voluntarily obligated herself to me, and I was delighted.

I was also downright possessive. Each coupon represented a future blessing. With them in my dresser, I felt like a capitalist with stacks of money in the bank or acres of property in my name. In short, I hoarded them.

In my opinion Abraham felt much the same. Hebrews 7:6 says that Abraham "had the promises." In other words he held deed to a few momentous words from God, including the guarantee that he would father a son, that his descendants would possess the land of Palestine, and that all peoples would be blessed through him. In five dramatic encounters, God, the great I Am, had voluntarily obligated Himself to a man of flesh and blood. Incredible.

Abraham responded fittingly. From then on, though materially prosperous, he regarded those promises as his treasured possession. Hoping in God's Word, he forsook home and country, journeyed to the Promised Land, wandered as a nomad, and waited for a miracle. He banked his waning future on words, to be sure, divine words.

For those who wonder, "Why go on?" God's promises become equally priceless. They are not a lottery ticket, a faint million-to-one chance, a desperate dream eventually tossed in the gutter. On the contrary, God's Word is absolutely reliable, backed up by the One "who cannot lie," says Titus 1:2 (NAS). If we feel secure investing in a bond rated AAA, how much more in a promise from God rated AAAAAAAAA . . . to infinity.

Vince and Teri thank God for the invaluable resource of first-rate doctors and hospitals, yet the medical institution was ultimately not their most precious asset. "I look back now and wonder," says Teri. "How in the world did we survive? I know it was because of the Word of God. I had never drawn so close to it before. The Bible that I used when Rebekah was going through this is torn in pieces, underlined everywhere. At the hospital when someone once handed me *Glamour* magazine, I said, 'I don't have time to read those; I have to read my Bible.' I didn't want to watch TV. I didn't want to spend a second away from meditating on the Word and singing Scripture songs because it was the only thing that really sustained me. Once you get away from the Word, all you have is hopeless thoughts."

Even the corps d'elite of doctors know their limitations. At the beginning of the crisis, as Vince and Teri conferred with the surgeons, Vince asked point-blank what Rebekah's chances were. The doctor pointed to the ceiling, looked up, and said, "It's not in my hands."

Vince recalls, "He said that he had only seen or read about ten cases like Rebekah's in the last ten years. I asked how many had survived. He wouldn't even answer."

At such times we anxiously perceive our dearest resource. Face-to-face with the impossible, which would prove more valuable to Vince and Teri, a million dollars or the promises of God? The finest surgeons or Psalm 73:26, ". . . God is the strength of my heart and my portion forever"? Obviously our world, so infatuated with wealth, with "the Lifestyles of the Rich and Famous," is overlooking the biggest bonanza of all: "He has given us his very great and precious promises . . ." (2 Peter 1:4).

Yet a promise gives us something money can't buy. For those groping for a reason to persevere, feeling meaningless or hopeless, a promise from God represents nothing less than— the future. Only God can grant that.

How does the Lord bestow promises? Can we arbitrarily stake a claim on any Bible verse? A few simple guidelines will suffice. First, we must differentiate between various types of promises. Some apply broadly to everyone: ". . . whoever wishes, let him take the free gift of the water of life" (Revelation 22:17). Others more narrowly address those who meet certain conditions: "If you believe, you will receive whatever you ask for in prayer" (Matthew 21:22). Still others are personal, spoken to an individual in the Bible and therefore not necessarily available to everyone: "I am with you, and no one is going to attack and harm you . . ." (spoken to Paul in Acts 18:10). However, in like manner, God may whisper a personal promise to us from any portion of Scripture. The best way to describe this experience is with the words of the disciples on the road to Emmaus:

"Were not our hearts burning within us while he talked with us on the road and opened the Scriptures to us?" (Luke 24:32).

Finding a promise is not a rare occurrence. Those who dedicate hours to Bible reading will stumble over mounds of unburied treasure, for the number of promises relevant for believers outweighs anything available to Abraham. The only paupers are those who neglect the Bible. In the end, we choose our own spiritual standard of living.

Promises Can Be Squandered

Once we prosper with promises, however, the Bible has a conditional clause written in bold print: In order to realize these promises, we must have perseverance.

Saul's life offers a valuable warning. At the time Samuel anointed him to be king, he gave him this promise, "Once these signs are fulfilled, do whatever your hand finds to do, for God is with you" (1 Samuel 10:7). In effect this assurance meant that God would grant Saul success in his enterprises. Who wouldn't relish that?

Saul, however, was required to do things God's way, and there lay the potential stumbling block. The prophet Samuel instructed him specifically about an upcoming mission: "Go down ahead of me to Gilgal. I will surely come down to you to sacrifice burnt offerings and fellowship offerings, but you must wait seven days until I come to you and tell you what you are to do" (1 Samuel 10:8).

Saul's obedience was quickly, belligerently tested. The Philistines, with countless chariots and soldiers, trampled into the land. In response, Saul blew the trumpet, and Israeli patriots began massing at Gilgal. There they saw clearly the overwhelming advantage of the enemy powers. Losing heart, the would-be warriors started slinking away and hiding in caves. Meanwhile, Saul grew uncomfortable.

The crisis question: With each passing day spelling fewer troops, would he obey Samuel by sitting tight? Would Saul persevere in listening to God's direction, or under pressure, would he rashly take priestly matters into his own sweaty hands?

Minutes ultimately decided the day. Saul waited one week for Samuel, the time set earlier, but he was nowhere in sight. Now down to six hundred men and fearing they also would scatter, he wrongly assumed the prophet's role by presenting a burnt offering to the Lord to seek His favor. Just as he finished, Samuel arrived—right on schedule.

Those few impulsive minutes betrayed many serious faults in Saul. Samuel promptly rebuked him:

> You acted foolishly. . . . You have not kept the command the Lord your God gave you; if you had, he would have established your kingdom over Israel for all time. But now your kingdom will not endure; the Lord has sought out a man after his own heart and appointed him leader of his people, because you have not kept the Lord's command.
>
> 1 Samuel 13:13, 14

His character his undoing, one of the Bible's most tragic figures soon began his disintegration. Although in the battle that followed, Saul and Israel survived because of God's gracious help, later after another major failure by Saul, God left him. Failing to persevere in obedience, Saul squandered the riches God had intended. Promises, our doorways into the storerooms of God's bounty, hinge on steadfastness.

Never Treat a Gem Like a Rock

In February of 1988, at a gem and mineral bazaar in Tucson, Arizona, there was a fateful transaction. An amateur rock collector sold an egg-sized, violet-and-blue stone to a Texas gemologist for $10. Later, after months of rigorous appraisals, the gemologist made an announcement about his $10 rock: It was a 1,905-carat star sapphire with an estimated, uncut value of $2.28 million.

His good fortune was not just good luck. Says he, "I was used to handling rocks and saying, 'Yeah, that's a keeper,' or, 'That's no good.' "

What a difference between the two men. The gem specialist is a happy fellow. The amateur will never forget his lost fortune. (We will disregard for now the question of fairness.) What separates a rock hound from a gemologist, the amateur's $10 from the professional's $2.28 million, is an eye and feel for value.

To their lasting regret, many believers resemble the rock hound. They part with a gem—the promise of God—insensible to its ultimate value. Hebrews 10:35 says, "Do not throw away your confidence; it will be richly rewarded." We can, if we choose, throw away the promise, sell cheap, give up on our hope, resign ourselves to a miserable future. But non-persevering Christians disqualify themselves from God's greatest blessings.

How much better it is to have an eye and feel for value. God's promises are keepers. They are worth holding for as long as necessary—for a lifetime if need be—for someday, like a handful of jewels, those few momentous words from God will yield a fortune.

3
To Bear Fruit

When was the last time you were on hold? Perhaps you phoned a busy store to order a Christmas gift. Abruptly the stressed-out clerk asked, "Would you please hold?" and then, before you could object, there was a click . . . and tin-canned reindeer music. So you waited, helplessly wasting your time, frustrated by the uncertainty of how long this would take.

In many respects we feel the same way when struggling with a situation that demands perseverance. We may wonder, *Is God helping me silently or avoiding me intentionally? How long will He take? Is my life being wasted?*

Such feelings were painfully familiar to Tony and Barb. In high school they were sweethearts, he a star fullback on the football team, she an attractive coed. At age twenty they married, continuing the all-American love story.

But the real world tends to thicken any plot. To avoid the local factories, Tony attended electrical trade school and on the side learned car repair. Day and night he toiled at work, school, and the garage. In addition Barb recalls, "I had to get a night job, and so we didn't see each other at all. For the next six years I was lonely. I'd come home and he'd be working on the car all the time."

The situation was intolerable and the results predictable. Never known to be shy, she vented her steamed emotions loud and strong at Tony. They began quarreling regularly, and at least monthly all-out war ensued.

All this misery prompted several major changes. As an outlet, Barb pursued a new career in modeling. Despite the competition in her major-city market, she soon rose to the top. Meanwhile, Tony faced a dead end: "I was frustrated about my work. I felt that I should be doing something different. There was no peace, no satisfaction. I was just going through the motions." They decided to move to Chicago where Barb quit modeling and Tony broke into photography. He began as an assistant to an established professional.

The glamour was short-lived. Tony slaved eighty hours a week for $150. His overlord scorned everything he did, berating him from morning till night. Barb, who was once again terribly lonely at home, followed suit in a tearful tug-of-war for her husband's time. Meanwhile, financial pressures weighed heavier and heavier, with bills six months overdue. A new city and a new career had not mended their marriage.

Things were, in fact, punishingly worse. It got to the point where Tony and Barb battled daily for hours. "We would fight until four in the morning," says Barb. "I was watching wrinkles come on my face. I was aging overnight because the stress was so intense. I was just *so* frustrated, *so* frustrated with Tony. For a solid week I did nothing but scream at him. I felt he was ruining my life, totally ruining my life, and I was stuck with him. I couldn't divorce him because my family would not accept that."

It's little surprise that Tony felt no better. "In my mind I had reached the end. I had come to pack my bags. I knew I couldn't stay around there. I just felt worthless, and attacked on every side. I was devastated."

Meltdown was near and they knew it. In their heart of hearts neither wanted to sever the relationship. They believed in God and knew He hated divorce. Although lacking deep spiritual commitment, Tony and Barb had attended church weekly throughout most of their marriage and had even developed a growing friendship with a strong Christian, a modeling acquaintance named Tina. But where was God in all these troubles? Prayer seemed feeble. Saddled with an overwhelming feeling that their lives were being wasted, Tony and Barb had reached ground zero. Why go on with this marriage? With this career? With anything?

They are not the only ones puzzled. In the throes of equally painful frustrations you yourself may be wondering, does the Lord want me barren? Does He punch the hold button, like the clerk at the store, callously indifferent to the waste of my time and my life?

Fortunately the Bible offers answers. When such questions arise, there are five soul-enriching things we need to know about God.

God Has a Green Thumb

Barrenness torments deeply, relentlessly. It is a relationship that withers, a career that fizzles, a dream that evaporates. Barrenness is unrealized potential, unmet needs, unproductive work. In somber tones, barrenness sings a dirge of emptiness and yearning. The barren, with their fields blighted by disease or parched by drought, feel an overwhelming sense of disappointment and loss.

At such a time in my own life, I discovered a Scripture that changed my song. I had been pastoring the Chicago church for about four years. Even though I toiled over my sermons, prayed for hours, visited people, planned for the future, in short did everything I knew how to reach people for Christ and establish the church, up to this point we had done little more than survive. The Windy City was a Kansas dustbowl.

Sitting dejectedly in my closet-sized office one day, I picked up my Bible and began my daily pattern of devotional reading, which included five chapters in the Old and New testaments. Shifting on my hard, wooden chair, which we could not afford to replace, I flipped to Genesis and the story of Joseph, the great-grandson of Abraham.

By the morning light shining on the pages, I read about the telling birth of Joseph's sons, Manasseh and Ephraim. In those days a child's name carried a lot of freight, intentionally chosen to describe a situation in the parent's life, an attitude toward God, or a prediction of the child's future. The explanation given for Ephraim's name hit me like a thunderbolt: "The second son he named Ephraim [which sounds like the Hebrew for *twice fruitful*] and said, 'It is because God has made me fruitful in the land of my suffering' " (Genesis 41:52).

Out loud I repeated, "God has made me fruitful in the land of my suffering." At that moment these words sounded as sweet to me as any ever heard. For indeed I was suffering. I was dwelling in Egypt. I felt barren and dusty. Yet even here God could make me fruitful. Especially here, the place of scorching tribulation, God delighted to fulfill His grandest purposes.

In my soul I knew the Lord had telegraphed these words to me as a promise. In response I bowed my head and prayed,

"Jesus, make me fruitful in the land of my suffering. Give me Ephraim."

This was a fitting response. God ordained these Old Testament biographies and histories as examples for us. They are true parables, benchmarks of how to relate to God, models for how God works with us. And for those struggling to persevere despite barrenness, God molded Joseph's life as a critical prototype. Modern men and women can put their faith in what God promised an ancient Israelite.

It might be objected, "Society was different back then. I doubt if Joseph's situation was as hopeless as mine."

Recall, please, his saga. As a youth he had great expectations, for God had inspired prophetic dreams indicating that someday all would bow before him—heady stuff for a teenager. On top of that he was his father's manifest favorite, recipient of a designer jacket that made him the envy of his brothers. It appeared the world would be his oyster.

Until sharks gathered. Ten jealous men sold their own flesh and blood into slavery. As Joseph trudged beside grunting camels through the desert sand toward captivity in Egypt, how did he feel about his career path? Who would buy him? A sadistic tyrant? Would he spend his life herniating to haul pyramid stones? Home, family, and holidays were now passé. What about marriage? Probably not. Honor? A master doesn't honor slaves; he pounds them and assigns them the dirty work. Talk about a wasted life. In terms of his past dreams, the future looked bleak at best.

As it turned out he was brokered to an elite military man who treated him well: upbeat bleak. Soon the soldier recognized Joseph's extraordinary gifts and God's clear blessing and promoted him to be manager of his entire household. Well, this wasn't so bad after all.

Then another cruel turn. His master's wife tried and failed to lure Joseph into adultery, then turned on him, framed him, and had him dumped into a dungeon—a dark, filthy, stinking, rat-teeming cell. What an opportunity for networking! It looked as if Joseph's life would be, to use Hobbes's phrase, "nasty, brutish, and short."

These were supposed to be his take-the-world-by-storm years. The poor man was in his twenties—the age of health, robustness, romance, opportunity, excitement—yet here he was rotting in the shadows. I wonder what he thought about God's direction and the dreams received eons before. If anyone has ever had reason for disillusionment and doubt, it was Joseph.

Years crept pointlessly by. Four . . . five . . . six . . . seven . . . for a young man that is a long, long time.

Then, a dramatic reversal, the kind of thing that happens with the Almighty on your side. Pharaoh tossed all night with troubling dreams. The next day he heard about Joseph's ability to unravel them, summoned him to the palace, received the God-inspired interpretation, and promptly promoted Joseph to chief administrator, Egypt's number-two man, Vice Pharaoh. In an overnight fulfillment of his own long-ago dream, Joseph now saw people bowing before him.

Unforeseen blessings also came his way. Pharaoh gave him a wife, who bore him Manasseh and Ephraim (twice fruitful). And it was then, after Ephraim's birth, that Joseph uttered those words so meaningful to me: "God has made me fruitful in the land of my suffering."

Joseph moved from barren desert to lush garden, from wasteland to oasis. God does have a green thumb.

Joseph also portrays the second thing we need to know about God.

God Always Seeks Fruit

According to John 15:1, 2, God is a typical Gardener. After all the trouble of plowing soil, planting seeds, fertilizing, and cultivating, He expects a harvest. "This is to my Father's glory," said Jesus in John 15:8, "that you bear much fruit. . . ." So fruitfulness is always God's will, which explains why Joseph bore much fruit even in the land of his suffering. Call it FBO (Farming By Objective).

In God's plans you won't find barrenness on the bottom line. Yes, for a time we may experience loss, waste, uselessness—perhaps for a long time—but God utilizes such periods to make us even *more* fruitful in the end. He is pruning us, clipping off some branches in order to fortify the rest. Or He is allowing us to lie fallow, resting and rejuvenating the soil. At the moment it seems like a ruinous loss, but in the end we reap a bumper crop.

God's unswerving purpose—fruitfulness—is clear from the very beginning. "Then God said, 'Let the land produce vegetation: *seed-bearing* plants and trees on the land that bear fruit *with seed in it*, according to their various kinds.' And it was so. . . . And God saw that it was good" (Genesis 1:11, 12 italics added). In His creation-wisdom, God engineered living things containing seeds. He programmed every living thing to reproduce.

In a walk through the forest, you quickly recognize one characteristic of seeds: profusion. A few weeks ago at the park, I picked a seedpod from a milkweed plant. I pulled it open and counted the seeds, each attached to its silken "parachute" strands: 321 seeds (margin of error: 6). The plant had six pods, meaning it produced about 2,000 seeds. If each took root, you would have 4 million seeds next time, then 8 billion, and so on.

As well as seed profusion, God planned fruit bounty. Last fall at the home of my wife's parents, I couldn't help but notice the pregnant apple tree in their backyard. It being September, the apples were ripening and falling from the branches. Although the ground was already covered and others had been picked and gathered, the tree was groaning under the weight of its produce, the branches bending to the ground. God has certainly created a world where fruitfulness is the copious watchword.

What about God's highest creation? Genesis 1:27 says, "God created man in his own image. . . ." In what ways does man resemble God? If we knew nothing about God and decided to learn about Him starting at page 1 of the Bible, we would immediately be impressed by His creativity, productivity, and fruitfulness. It is no surprise, then, what God's *first* recorded words to man are: "Be fruitful and increase in number; fill the earth and subdue it . . ." (Genesis 1:28). Like Father like son and daughter.

By commanding one thing, God reveals His antipathy for its opposite. And in fact the Lord does scorn barrenness. Note for example this parable of Jesus:

A man had a fig tree, planted in his vineyard, and he went to look for fruit on it, but did not find any. So he said to the man who took care of the vineyard, "For three years now I've been coming to look for fruit on this fig tree and haven't found any. Cut it down! Why should it use up the soil?"

"Sir," the man replied, "leave it alone for one

more year, and I'll dig around it and fertilize it. If it
bears fruit next year, fine! If not, then cut it down."

Luke 13:6–9

Such a parable can sorely discourage those who, like a determined apple tree in a scorching desert, are trying but failing to bear fruit. So what's the point? Why the emphasis on
God's enthusiasm for fruitfulness? Because when seeking God
to deliver us from a time that seems wasted, we must know
our prayer pleases Him. We can be absolutely certain that
when praying for fruitfulness in the land of suffering, we are
praying according to His will.

Why, then, the delay? Why did Abraham have to wait
twenty-five years for Isaac if Isaac was God's will? Why must
some of us persevere for months, years, or decades in seeming
futility?

God Thought Up the Law of the Harvest

These are big questions, with a miniscule answer. We find
it in Genesis 1: "Let the land produce vegetation: *seed-bearing
plants*. . . ." All life—plant, animal, and human—comes from
little seeds (the Greek word for "seed" is *sperma*). The life
cycle of plant seeds begins with a disappearing act under the
ground. To the eye, they are dead and gone. In reality a
miracle is in progress. The seed germinates; eventually a
seedling sprouts. Similarly, in humans there is conception,
nine months of gestation, then birth. The tyrannous little
truism: Fruitfulness depends on seeds, and seeds take time.

A man must obey the law of the land. Standing on the black
soil of central Illinois, a farmer rips open a bag of corn seed
and pours the golden nuggets into a planter. He mounts his

tractor and begins crisscrossing the fields, mechanically jamming the hard seeds into the dirt. The job done, he wipes his sweaty brow, drags into the house, and turns his mind to other projects. Nothing he can do can speed the process. Now it's up to the sun, the rain, the warm earth, the seeds. For a while he sees only furrows. Then green blades. Inch by inch the crop stands ever taller until finally, the harvest, when the farmer reaps the benefit of his investment. All told, months of patient waiting between sowing and reaping. It is the law of the harvest, worked in soil, etched in stone.

This rocky decree yields invisible blessings. In addition to being the unbending harvest law of the physical realm, sowing and reaping also govern the spiritual. This should encourage us. Remember, after creating plants with seeds "God saw that it was good." In the spiritual realm, it is likewise pleasing. We disparage God's wisdom if we impatiently view the harvest model as unfortunate but necessary red tape. It is God's quintessential design, and one reason why we must wait for the fruitfulness that God so strongly intends.

God Can Bless Only Patient Farmers

God won't bless just anybody. Since He designed the law of the harvest, only the farmer who can cope with its time factor can benefit. No one succeeds by running feverishly into a field of three-inch seedlings and yelling, "Lord, if You don't give me a harvest tomorrow, I give up on this crop." If Joseph had turned bitterly away from God, he would have lacked the divine inspiration to interpret Pharaoh's dream and rise to power. He was fruitful in the land of his suffering because he was steadfast in the ways of his God. It is the persevering farmer who qualifies for fruitfulness.

We are all, in effect, spiritual tillers of the soil. James 5:7, 8 says, "Be patient, then, brothers, until the Lord's coming. See how the farmer waits for the land to yield its valuable crop and how patient he is for the autumn and spring rains. You too, be patient and stand firm. . . ." Notice two nutrients in this verse:

1. *The farmer works in partnership with nature: with the land, with the autumn and spring rains.* In like manner, the Christian sharecrops with God. It doesn't all depend on us. We have a bountiful resource—the soil of the kingdom of God—more fertile than anything on earth. As a result the Lord sometimes wants us simply to pray about our concerns and then to watch the soil, sun, showers, and seeds of the kingdom do their work. By persevering, with prayer and faith, we allow time and space for God's miracles.

2. *Waiting is part of the farmer's job description.* He works by waiting. And it's hard work. For instance, as we sit endlessly in the doctor's reception area or stand in a long line at the bank, many of us blow fuses. But despite the difficulty, waiting is the work of the spiritual farmer, the challenging regimen of any fruitful Christian: "God . . . acts on behalf of those who wait for him" (Isaiah 64:4).

There is one final thing that we, who feel as if the hold button has been pushed in heaven, need to know about God.

God Guarantees the Law of the Harvest

We can learn something else about the law of the harvest from, of all places, Davy Jones's locker.

Sailing is a risky business. A Spanish galleon, the *Atocha*, was bound for home after collecting the treasures of the Indies, South America, and Central America. As the rear guard of a twenty-eight-vessel flotilla, the *Atocha* bristled with twenty bronze cannons, and its hold was laden with gold and silver bars, ingots, chains, and ornaments, as well as precious household utensils like a solid gold spoon.

But those twenty cannons were useless against their worst enemy on September 6, 1622. In the Gulf of Mexico that's hurricane season. A savage one pummeled the ships, sweeping them toward the Florida coast. Near the Marquesas Keys, eight of the vessels, including the *Atocha*, foundered and sank to the bottom.

They rested in peace for 365 years. Come the 1980s, a deep-sea treasure hunter took up the scent. With the aid of a college professor who pored over Spanish archival documents of the ill-fated voyage, he discovered what is now considered perhaps the greatest underwater archaeological find of the century: the wreckage of the *Atocha*, complete with its cargo worth millions.

But the most remarkable discovery on the *Atocha* may not be gold and silver. As others in the salvage crew counted the booty, an archaeologist sifted the sand and gravel that had once been the ballast. He found fascinating things (to archaeologists anyway) such as fish bones, insect parts, sawdust . . . and seeds.

In fact, 250 varied seeds. To keep them from drying out, he put them in cups of fresh water. Checking the water level nine days later, he made his own discovery. "Suddenly, I saw leaves sticking up." To his astonishment, 4 of the 365-year-old seeds had sprouted.

Seeds have power. Longevity. Life.

Even more virile are spiritual seeds. God has promised,

". . . A man reaps what he sows" (Galatians 6:7). Our words and deeds and prayers—all of which are seeds—will one day be harvested. If the seeds of this corruptible world can last for centuries, how much more the incorruptible seeds of the spiritual realm.

There is another rule of agriculture, though, equally powerful, that qualifies the law of the harvest, namely, the law of the farmer. Galatians 6:9 says, "Let us not become weary in doing good, for at the proper time we will reap a harvest *if we do not give up*" (italics added). From this verse we glean three agricultural principles:

1. *If we quit, we lose the harvest.* Notice in the verse that the harvest is conditioned by that small but crucial word *if*. Spiritual seeds can perish, and their greatest threat is the planter. God won't destroy them. We, by giving up, kill seeds.

2. *If we persevere, we can bank on fruit.* In this world, farmers get accustomed to uncertainty. But the harvest of the spiritual world is certain for the steadfast. Even when Satan unleashes his most terrible pests, instead of causing crop failure, they work, in the long run, like fertilizer. Jesus proved that at the cross.

3. *Our biggest enemies are weariness and despair.* Chances abound for a letdown. Granted, doing God's will is worthwhile and exciting, but also exhausting at times and potentially discouraging. Although in our urban era we romanticize it, farm work is tedious. To change the metaphor, a heavyweight boxer in the final rounds battles not only his counterpart in the ring but also the fatigue in his flesh. More than anyone else we fight ourselves, the enemy within.

Which brings us back to Tony and Barb, with their marriage on the canvas.

It was a brisk, gray, fall day. After one week of pitched conflict, both sides were war weary. In order to get out of the house, Barb called her friend Tina. She slipped on her coat, hurried down the stairs, and walked seven blocks to a neighborhood park, a small island of green within the city, where they met. Sitting on a bench with Tina, Barb poured out her woes for the next hour. She reviewed the whole situation, the problems, the attempts to solve them, the hopelessness. After listening quietly for an hour, Tina had only one question: "You've tried everything else; why not try Jesus?"

Barb paused. "You're right, I have tried everything else, but I haven't tried the Jesus you've got."

Quietly they got up from the bench, and Barb walked home deep in thought. She climbed the stairs to their second-floor apartment, entered the living room, and sat down at a table. The battle lines were still drawn, with Tony pacing the apartment, packing to go who knows where. Finally Barb said, "Tony, you have to accept Jesus with me. We can't go on like this."

For the first time in a week, he made no angry retort. Her words struck something deep inside, and he simply knew she was right. "If you're for real," he said, "I'll do it." He sat down beside her, took her hands, and together they bowed their heads. "Jesus, please come into our lives," Barb prayed, "and help our marriage."

That was all. They talked quietly for a little while, about how to follow Jesus in the manner that Tina did, and then they went on about their work. The seven-day war was over.

The first change noticed by both was a new conscience. "When we got upset with each other," says Barb, "and I started to raise my voice or yell something, I felt a deep sense of conviction come over me, and I could sense that he did, too. It was as if we were hearing our own words for the first time, and they weren't godly."

Although utopia didn't suddenly dawn, they also noticed a dramatic reversal in attitude. For the first time in years, instead of emptiness "there was hope," says Tony. "We knew that with God there is always hope."

"That hope," continues Barb, "got us through the infancy stages of our Christianity." Jesus enabled them to better endure the friction that nonetheless lingered, while He gradually rubbed away their sharp edges.

Though major repairs still needed to be done, at least Tony and Barb had been towed out of the ditch and onto the road, a long road with hills yet to climb, but a road that led somewhere.

God's ultimate will is not failure. He doesn't want our lives wasted, and He doesn't forget or avoid us, even when we feel as though we're on hold. If we get close to Him, the Lord of the harvest, there is fruitfulness in our future.

4
To Develop Christlikeness

Few things cause more distress for new Christians than their own weaknesses. For example, after dedicating my life to Christ as a college sophomore, I battled with old habits and problems. On bad days I would thirst to drink beer again. At times I wrestled with doubts, depression, or fear. I won some and, to my anguish, lost some.

Taking a seat in a church pew can be like going to the dugout after a strikeout. But far from resenting my teammates, I was in awe of the home-run hitters in our congregation. Our pastor had incomparable faith and dedication. Ron, the worship leader, beamed with joy. Our adult Sunday school teacher was the most loving person I had ever met. Kurt, a board member, was as stable as the Rock of Gibraltar. In these men, I recognized greatness, and the source of that greatness: Jesus Christ. Increasingly, I wanted to be like Jesus.

Eagerly I applied myself to growing in Christ. Having heard about the importance of Bible reading and prayer, I established a disciplined devotional life, actually without much difficulty. I quickly learned to cherish my time with the Lord and devoured the Scriptures like a starving man.

But I wasn't so eager when God began His own regimen of spiritual training in my life. In fact, disappointment and distaste would better describe my response. Although it uniquely interwove and applied the spinnings of my devotional life and church involvement, the program hardly felt spiritual. Eventually I learned that it was, nonetheless, scriptural, clearly outlined in James 1:3, 4:

> . . . the testing of your faith develops perseverance.
> Perseverance must finish *its work*
> so that you may be *mature and complete,*
> *not lacking anything* (italics added).

My chagrin at God's training program would have been less had I better understood this verse, and from it three encouraging truths about the relationship between Christlikeness and perseverance.

Perseverance Makes Us Muscular, Not Musclebound

Perseverance is high-tech training. Perhaps you have exercised on a Nautilus machine. With pulleys, pads, and hinges, it targets specific muscle groups for stress, demanding a constant exertion over a full range of motion. Such state-of-the-art design, coupled with old-fashioned sweat, builds power. In like manner, perseverance requires the strenuous exertion of the very muscles, weak and unused, that we prefer to ignore. It demands something out of us while putting spiritual fiber into us. What the obstacle is doesn't matter much, as long as perseverance is required.

Perseverance uniquely conditions us to be muscular, not musclebound, through balanced character training. Notice the two dimensions of spiritual fitness described in James 1:4:

1. *Maturity.* Perseverance is a rite of passage through which we move from spiritual adolescence to adulthood. By steadfastness we come of age in responsibility, holiness, wisdom, judgment, prayer, faith, love, hope. A mature believer, like a full-grown apple tree, produces a bountiful crop of the fruits of the Spirit and of unselfish ministry.

2. *Completeness.* This means there is nothing lacking, in contrast with those who are mature yet incomplete, like a five-year-old fruit-bearing tree missing three severed branches. The complete have both faith and works, knowledge and wisdom, strength and mercy, zeal and patience, enthusiasm and self-control.

The combination of maturity and completeness is a rare commodity. For example, major league baseball abounds with mature pitchers who know the hitters, how to change speeds, whether to throw a fastball or a curve, and how to attack a hitter's weakness, but after ten years in the league, they've lost the pop on their fastball. Conversely, plenty of rookies sport a blistering fastball, a handcuffing slider, and even a change-up, yet hitters pound them out of the park because they are throwers ignorant of the art of pitching. Mature and complete hurlers go to the Hall of Fame.

Greatness of character, both mature and complete, eludes us in some common ways. Believers may know a lot but do very little. We might love everyone yet lust for the sinful world, study the Bible yet neglect prayer. Unfortunately, we can be very "holy" but stingy, gifted but fickle, zealous but foolhardy.

Why are Hall of Famers the exception rather than the rule? Clearly our Christlikeness is God's will. With all the resources He has provided—the Bible, the anointing, the example of Christ, the church, books and magazines, prayer—why aren't mature and complete believers commonplace?

Because too often we shrink from perseverance. In pursuit of Christlikeness, we prefer training centers, degrees from colleges, credentials from a denomination, or seminars by big-name leaders. All these are beneficial but no replacement for the longer path described in James 1:4.

Tony and Barb, who survived so much combat before accepting Jesus into their lives and marriage, found that maturity and completeness come more gradually than salvation. Although Jesus gave them bright, sure hope, He did not suddenly solve all their problems.

In fact, a new venture soon multiplied them. Barb began a business of her own, shooting composite photos for models. Before long her success enabled Tony to quit his unrewarding job, and a husband-wife team was born.

Teamwork, however, scarcely described their relationship. "That first experience of working together was tough," says Tony. "Even though we had given our hearts to the Lord, we still had some very difficult emotions to work through because both of us had been hurt by each other so deeply. On top of that we were both independent, stubborn people. Working together was never a piece of cake for us."

Yet they did complement each other professionally. Barb handled models, scheduling, organization, and front work, while Tony concentrated on the technical aspects. What they lacked was a proven, professional image. They moved up, for the gourmet touch, to another studio, which doubled as their apartment, appropriately large, nice—and expensive. The pressure to succeed went up with them.

Then, the clincher: Barb became pregnant, and the stress mounted intolerably. Physical changes, emotional swings, a thick pile of bills, an uncertain business, preparation for a second child—all combined for a resurgence in squabbling, often in front of clients, the very clients they had been telling about Jesus and inviting to a weekly Bible study. Feeling increasingly ashamed of her Christian testimony and over-whelmed by the situation, Barb dropped out of the business.

Without her, Tony was in wide-angle-lens trouble. He felt abandoned. Their marriage polarized, with Barb seeking refuge in God and Tony reaching his wit's end over bills, business, and survival. Boiling with anger and resentment, Tony occasionally erupted with volcanic fury.

"I remember times," says Barb, "of lying in bed trying to go to sleep, while Tony was screaming at me in frustration. He had frustrations that weren't mine anymore. I had figured out how to get my peace in the Lord before he had."

Tony only knew he felt alone. He interpreted Barb's peace as indifference and, worse yet, wondered about his relation-ship with God. "When I was there at the bottom, in the deepest of debt, I was trying to figure out whether God liked me anymore. I wondered whether He would help me out of that big hole I'd dug for myself or whether I was going to debtor's prison. I mean, I didn't know where I was."

Why all the problems? Now, with some distance and per-spective, Tony and Barb see quite clearly where they were. "I didn't grow the way God wanted," says Tony. "I sort of held back. There was some rebellion in me."

"For both of us there was a problem with selfish ambition," admits Barb. "That was the root of the conflict."

On the other hand, they also had good roots sunk fairly deep in the Lord. So far these had not withered. They would prove decisive.

Perseverance Develops Christlikeness in Four Unique Ways

How does perseverance generate Christlikeness? Aren't there more efficient ways? Shouldn't Bible study, prayer, self-evaluation, and self-discipline suffice?

We can find answers by looking at the sport of running. A devotee of marathons can read all the magazines and books, talk with fellow enthusiasts, watch races, study the physiology and chemistry of his body, monitor his diet, and set inspirational goals for himself—but if he fails to actually run daily, he will remain a well-sneakered spectator. Perseverance at God's will does something unique, something that synthesizes the other disciplines. Four special things happen.

1. *Perseverance exercises the muscle of the soul.* Consider how marathoners differ from sprinters. Hundred-yard dashers charge up emotionally for a ten-second explosion. They run on powerful legs and are often high-strung personalities. Marathoners, on the other hand, don't run on their legs or emotions; they run on their will. For five and six hours a day in training, then for more than two hours in the race, they scissor one gnarled leg in front of another, intent on their goal despite pain, exhaustion, delirium, and weakness. By over-

coming their body's resistance mile after mile, marathoners exercise their will as much as their legs and lungs. The result: an emaciated-looking body and a will—if you could see it— like Charles Atlas.

In a Christian, when such willpower is properly directed to forcefully will God's will, it energizes noble character.

Consider the mushy alternative. A weak will means instability, a habit of being guided by feelings rather than wisdom. Paul speaks of people who are "weak-willed . . . swayed by all kinds of evil desires . . ." (2 Timothy 3:6). James describes someone who "is like a wave of the sea, blown and tossed by the wind. That man should not think he will receive anything from the Lord; he is a double-minded man, unstable in all he does" (James 1:6–8).

The cure for spiritual schizophrenia is perseverance.

"That's a catch-22," someone objects. "How can I persevere if I have a weak will? That's like asking a lame man to walk."

No, it's like asking a one-year-old to *learn* to walk. Toddlers gain the strength to crawl, then walk, by struggling and trying. It comes gradually. And that is the genius of perseverance. Spiritual fibers thicken with each decision to hang on for one more minute, one more hour, one more day. *Perseverance transforms* a double-minded, unstable person into a single-minded follower of God's will.

2. *Perseverance conditions us to choosing the long-term, difficult way over the short-term, easy way.* Recall again the marathon runner. He or she habitually chooses the hard way, straining toward a distant goal and ignoring immediate comforts. That mind-set typifies the growing Christian. We embrace today the rigors of doing right for the sake of God's approval at

Judgment Day. We resist temptation, put our hope in God's coming kingdom, stockpile treasures in heaven, and anticipate the physical return of Jesus instead of indulging the sinful passions and pleasures of the moment. Athletes and Christians think in terms of delayed rewards.

Tony and Barb discovered something during their marital struggles. "There is no choice. With the Lord you either persevere or you go backward. You can choose what *seems* the easy way, or you choose the hard way, which ends up being the easy way. I have found that by running from trials you end up on the harder road in the long run. You must face it. You must face and work through it with the Word of God as a guide."

3. *Perseverance sends our roots deeper into God.* The depth of a plant's root system varies according to the need. With regular, abundant rain, a tree's roots can be shallow, but in a drought they grow deep into the soil for water. Similarly, with prosperity we may lack the drive to deepen our relationship with the Lord. When life dries out like a desert, though, and we verge on collapsing face-first into the sand, suddenly we can't get enough of Jesus. Panting for His promises, encouragement, and fellowship, we read the Bible thirstily, pray continually, and attend church devotedly. The deeper our roots go into God, the more living water we drink, which stimulates Christlikeness: "The fruit of the Spirit is love, joy, peace, patience, kindness, goodness, faithfulness, gentleness and self-control . . ." (Galatians 5:22, 23).

In my own life I have written proof of this phenomenon. In one section of my daily planning book, I jot down devotional thoughts and inspirations from my Bible reading. I write only when something special hits me. Looking back over the last couple of years, I find the greatest frequency of entries clustering in difficult times when perseverance was sorely tested. Those insights have always prompted spiritual growth.

4. *Perseverance forces us to sort our values, priorities, and goals.* None of us repeatedly does what is difficult without some legitimate reason. In fact without compelling objectives, we all behave like water: taking the path of least resistance. Why persevere if you can quit? Face-to-face with a huge challenge, we are forced to know our reasons for going on, to sort and clarify what really matters, what is worth suffering for.

Such assessments take various, painful shapes. Under attack from her family for her recent conversion, a nineteen-year-old college student decides that Jesus means more to her than even her own flesh and blood, so she resolves to continue attending church. In a struggle with recurring sexual temptation, a divorced man reasons that an eternal heaven is more important than today's passing erotic pleasure, and so he once again says no to pornography. Although such individuals may not know how they'll go on, they do know *why* they'll go on.

A tough day on the job helped one man sort his priorities. He was a commodities trader. During a one-on-one discipleship meeting, his pastor challenged him to give the next day's earnings in the pit to overseas missions. The next day turned out to be a sluggish downer in the market. Nevertheless, he scrambled, screamed, wheeled, and dealed. At the closing bell, as he turned in his trading tickets, the clerk remarked, "How on earth did you make this much money on a day when the market went nowhere?" He had made more than a thousand dollars.

He knew how and why. Later that night on the phone, his voice hoarse, he told his pastor, "That is the most satisfying day I have ever had. I never would have done what I did today for money. Only for Jesus."

Instead of being like water, which follows the path of least resistance, perseverance makes us like fire. We burn hotter and fiercer if trees stand in our way. We thrive on resistance. We travel faster uphill than downhill, in a windstorm than a lull. History has shown that believers flame bright with adversity and flame out in prosperity.

Perseverance definitely forced Tony and Barb to sort their agenda. It was December, a cheerful time of year, but not for Tony. Financially and professionally the year had proved disastrous, leaving them $15,000 in debt, due immediately. One night, sitting at the kitchen table with Barb after the kids had gone to bed, Tony finally voiced what he had been thinking for weeks: "I can't keep going on like this. I have to find out whether this Bible really works or not. I've tried relying on myself when it comes to business, and it's gotten me nowhere. Now I'm going to try putting God first."

Several weeks earlier a Scripture had caught Tony's attention and been unavoidable since then. "Seek ye first the kingdom of God, and his righteousness; and all these things shall be added unto you" (Matthew 6:33 KJV). For the first time in his Christian experience, he was going to bet his financial future on it.

Barb supported his conviction. There in the kitchen of their tiny rear apartment they prayed, dedicating themselves to doing whatever God wanted, however God wanted. Then they asked the Lord to miraculously provide $15,000.

January came, and Tony had no clients. One day his pastor called. "Tony, while you're not working, how about doing some of the remodeling we need here at the church? I know the pay is peanuts, but we can only afford five dollars an hour."

Decision time. Should he say no and keep scrambling for clients (his only hope for a debt-paying bonanza) or work for God? His pastor's offer seemed like no coincidence; it appeared the Lord wanted to see if he meant what he had prayed. "I'll be there Tuesday morning," Tony later told his pastor.

For four weeks he sawed two-by-fours, nailed Sheetrock, and spread paint for twenty to thirty hours a week in addition to doing small photo jobs.

It was now February in Chicago, cold and forbidding. At five o'clock one Friday afternoon as Tony sat at his bill-cluttered desk, his Radio Shack telephone pulsed. It was a photographer's rep he had met through a mutual friend six weeks earlier. In her aggressive, keeping-track-of-a-thousand-things voice, she asked if he was interested in some work the very next day. Her usual photographer was booked, and this was one of her big clients, Citicorp Bank.

"You bet I'm interested," said Tony. He hung up the phone and spent the night pulling together equipment. Somehow he scratched up the money to buy film. At nine-thirty the next morning he hauled his camera bags into McCormick Place, Chicago's main convention center, where he worked a long and successful Saturday. In fact, it was the best-paying job Tony had ever had, grossing $3,000 in one day.

And it was only the beginning. They admired his artistry and asked him to continue. Over the next three weeks Tony worked sixty hours and earned another $9,000 net. That job ended and in successive order others came, each paying $1,000 or more. Within two months Tony cleared $17,000.

From his desk, the bill pile disappeared. Matthew 6:33 proved to be money in the bank.

A major obstacle still loomed, however. Tony and Barb had enjoyed periods of financial prosperity before without any decrease in friction.

Following another year of continued marital stress, the breakthrough finally came. "After six years of slow growth," says Barb, "God told me to just focus on seeking Him. At the same time I felt strongly impressed to read through the Matthew Henry Commentaries. For the next year, in the morning and afternoon while my kids took their naps, I would sit down at the kitchen table, pull out the thick, black commentary, and slowly read, pondering first the Scripture and then Henry's comments.

"He stressed piety and godliness over and over again. Through 1,600 pages in one year I was saturated with the theme of godly living. I never would have believed that reading a commentary could transform a person, but it did, dramatically. And as I changed, so did our marriage. As I began responding to situations in Christlike fashion, whether Tony was right or wrong, we began to get along, and it motivated him to treat me better."

Perseverance Eventually Yields a Masterpiece

Is Christlike character worth the pain? "I'm happy the way I am," someone claims. "I don't hurt or steal from anybody. I'm not cheating on my wife. Why should I have to go through all this heartbreak just to get a little more patience or humility? There's a lot worse people than me in the world, and they're not going through the troubles I am." From our vantage point, precious few things merit suffering.

But what about God's perspective? How does He feel about our character? To understand that, we first must remember that He created us. How would Michelangelo feel about a glob of tar on the ceiling of the Sistine Chapel? Or Frederic Remington about dirty rags draped on his statue *The Bronco Buster?* Great artists cherish their masterpieces, sometimes above all else.

God is the Artist of artists. After a six-day period of dazzling, prolific creativity, He fashioned His crowning work: a modified self-portrait—man. Neither glowing sunset nor majestic mountain could compare with the nobility of those who reflected God's righteousness, creativity, authority, rational thinking, love. After molding man into the world scene, instead of repeating that the creation was good, as He had done previously, God pronounced, "it was *very* good." A Genius and His tour de force.

A piece of art is a fragile thing. Like the statue of the *Pietà*, defaced in 1972 by a hammer-wielding madman, God's creation was promptly vandalized. The serpent seduced Adam and Eve, tarring innocence with sin, shame, hatred, fear, and doubt. To the Creator, the masterpiece was now profoundly repulsive.

But God is a persistent Genius. Instead of destroying the eyesore in rage, in love He chose to painstakingly restore man to his former glory. Thus, He sent His Son to earth, not merely to rewrite His name in the corner of the painting, but to perfectly and absolutely renew man to his destined greatness. As Romans 8:29 says, "He also predestined [us] to be *conformed to the likeness of his Son . . .*" (italics added). This renewed likeness for man, as we would expect from so great an Artist, outshines by far the original masterpiece.

After this monumental investment in restoration, the Lord

will spare no price in completing the work. He comes to live inside us—although we are still beset by displeasing sins—in order to help us change. He intercedes for our maturation continually. He commands His shepherds to train disciples. If our Christlikeness is that worthwhile to God, it is no less for us. By persevering we invest in a priceless commodity.

We, after all, are the greatest beneficiaries. Life hums along more smoothly with maturity, as Tony and Barb have discovered. Perseverance and Christlikeness have given them a relationship they never thought possible. "We now enjoy one another the way we used to when we first met," says Barb. "We go out on a date once a week, sometimes just walking and talking for a couple of hours. I have gotten the desire of my heart from my husband. I'm completely happy and satisfied. I don't see what more God could do. But if you had talked to me three years ago, I would have wished it was all over."

Perseverance accomplishes some pretty amazing things. It exercises the muscle of the soul, conditions us to choosing long-term benefits, sends our roots deeper into God, and clarifies our values and goals. Perseverance lifts us to uncommon heights of maturity. Perseverance, perhaps the most unspiritual and mundane-feeling aspect of the Christian life, produces results as great and exalted and spiritual as the reflection of Christ Himself. And to our surprise, it sooner or later makes us profoundly happy.

5
To Synchronize
With the Season

A season is a dominating thing. A season is thus difficult to ignore. One sunny day some chums gathered for a swim. As you would expect, they sported their beach towels, caps, and trunks, and one by one, in less than championship style, they dove in. "Beautiful day for a dip," several shouted.

But try as they might, they couldn't kick back and relax, for this was Lake Michigan in January. Vapor clouds hung over the icy waters. The TV newsmen who covered the story stood shivering in coats, hats, boots, and gloves. This annual gathering certainly ranks as one of the most exclusive clubs in town, an exception that proves the rule: Seasons prevail.

Consider another odd seasonal situation, this one hypothetical. It is October in the breadbasket of America. In one farmer's field stands a gold mine of corn. On adjacent fields, his neighbors' combines are crawling through the harvest, picking diligently before bad weather spells ruin. But this man's combine sits quietly in the barn. After harvesting several acres, he had tired and impetuously decided to vacation in Florida, where he now lounges beside a swimming pool, sipping lemonade.

These two stories illustrate the same thing: someone out of synch with the season. Although offbeat examples, they nevertheless reflect some of our own inclinations. Like the Polar Bear Club, we sometimes act inappropriately given the prevailing climate. Or like the farmer, we squander a golden opportunity. Either way, we lurch ineptly out of rhythm with the season.

The result is frustration, fruitlessness, and failure. Spiritually we bog down and wonder why God's Word seemingly fails. We may flit from one interest to another, never achieving solid, lasting results. Like a four-year-old at the mall, we either dash ahead or lag behind the Lord, finding ourselves both exhausted and disappointed.

How can we synchronize with the seasons of life? How can we maximize ripe time? How can we keep in step with God in our career, family, ministry, and finances?

Recognize God's Ordained Seasons

First, we need to open our eyes to God's activity. Though less easily observed than a thunderhead blowing out of the Gulf of Mexico, to the searching eye it is, nevertheless, perceptible. Too often we simply charge ahead, oblivious to God's spiritual seasons, like the eccentric who trudges through the snow without coat or boots. Regrettably, we suffer similar consequences.

Frostbite nipped me in 1988. Several months after moving from Chicago to Arlington Heights, our church went through a time of severe barrenness. I grew increasingly discouraged and began wondering if we had somehow missed God's will. Surely this served no good purpose. In search of some guiding light, I spent extra time seeking God, and He soon brought to my attention Scriptures such as 1 Peter 5:6, "Humble yourselves, therefore, under God's mighty hand, that he may lift you up in due time." It dawned on me that this was a season for humility, a time to wait on God, to fast and kneel before Him. In so doing, before long I sensed breakthrough, and the situation gradually reversed. In retrospect I saw that the key to my fruitful passage through this season was the recognition of the Lord's spiritual objective.

But does God always have a seasonal purpose? For every situation? For what we are going through today?

These questions are answered unequivocally in three Scripture passages:

> It is God who works in you to will and to act according to his good purpose.
>
> Philippians 2:13

> In all things God works for the good of those who love him. . . .
>
> Romans 8:28

> He who began a good work in you will carry it on to completion until the day of Christ Jesus.
>
> Philippians 1:6

Clearly, God is anything but disengaged. From these verses we note two faith-building principles.

1. *God always has a good purpose.* He is never at a loss for worthwhile projects with us. Even when life just feels like a

long line to the checkout clerk, God focuses relentlessly, intensively on eternal objectives. He never says, "I'll get back to you in two months. Kill a little time for me." Or, "I can't think of anything significant to work on right now." The countless ways that we need to grow and the innumerable needs for our service in the lives of others can easily fill any to-do list. In fact, if we knew all the things the Lord could be working on, we would find that the agenda for any one moment is merely His micro-short list.

2. *God persists unflaggingly in that purpose.* The Lord seeks to finish what He begins. Therefore, He never gives up, never gets tired. To say God is determined would be one of the greatest understatements of all time. No matter how wasted our lives may seem, if we are seeking Him, we can be sure purpose and meaning abound.

These two principles underscore a key insight for the cure of spiritual blindness. *Because of God's purposes*, life has spiritual seasons—winter, spring, summer, and fall. God's purposes are the jet stream directing our "weather patterns." Ecclesiastes 3:1, 2 says, "There is a time for everything, and a season for every activity under heaven: a time to be born and a time to die, a time to plant and a time to uproot." Rather than the year-round sunny climate of Southern California, life resembles the ever-changing weather of the Midwest. Clouds come and go. Temperatures rise and fall. It's windy, then sunny, snowy, then hot. In all the changes, the discerning Christian looks for God.

In spiritual weather watching, a thermometer is more important than a wristwatch. To describe time, the original language of the New Testament uses two different words.

Chronos describes time as measured by the clock. You may recognize it as the root of our English words *chronometer, chronicle, chronic*, and *chronological. Chronos* measures the *quantity* of time.

The other word, *kairos,* generally describes time in terms of its characteristics, its *qualities* rather than quantity, the kinds of things better measured with a weathervane, barometer, or rain meter. *Kairos* is often translated "season," which is, of course, a period of time with certain distinctive features. In 2 Corinthians 6:2, for example, God says, " 'In the *time* of my favor I heard you, and in the day of salvation I helped you.' I tell you, now is the *time* of God's favor, now is the day of salvation" (italics added). Here the Greek word translated "time" is *kairos.* In other words, the Lord's open-door policy will endure for only a season. This is a limited period of time with definite characteristics, a fleeting season of opportunity to find everlasting mercy, forgiveness, and salvation. Those who ignore it will miss their chance, die without Christ, and be lost forever. Clearly, a weather eye for the signs of the times is of no small consequence.

God has equipped us with more than the naked eye. Our primary meteorological instrument is the Bible, which clearly reveals God's objectives, God's will, and God's ways and teaches how to respond accordingly in every climate.

In addition to recognizing God's ordained seasons there is a second requirement for making the most of ripe time.

Work Persistently While Time Is Ripe

Several years ago, on a drive through central Illinois on a cool fall night, I got a mild surprise. It was about ten-thirty.

Glancing to my left into the darkness I spotted a pair of head-lights weaving through a farm field. At first I assumed it was a pick-up on a dirt road, but then I realized it was a combine wending its way in the night through rows of corn.

This farmer was driven by more than insomnia or worka-holism. He recognized the harvest as a ticking bonanza. Once the season is right and the field dry, farmers toil around the clock before their gold turns to clay. Bonanzas also tick in the spiritual realm: "Be very careful, then, how you live—not as unwise but as wise, making the most of every *opportunity* . . ." (Ephesians 5:15, 16 italics added).

Dulled by the daily grind, we usually underestimate the number of ripe moments within our grasp. In this verse the word translated "opportunity" is *kairos,* which we just noted means season. So this could be rephrased, "Make the most of every season." What hope this gives to the person who sees no meaning in life. In God's sovereignty every moment is a season, and every season an opportunity. For the believer, life is always ripe to accomplish something for eternity that at another time could not be achieved.

But what is our inclination? In difficult seasons we tend to moan and grouse. We vent our spleen or soak in melancholy. Wanting to harvest corn, we scorn the soybeans ripe in the field. Setting our sights on temporal, worldly goals, we over-look the eternal payoffs within our grasp. The result is spiri-tual crop failure.

Successful farmers work with as much savvy and resource-fulness as any big-city entrepreneur. For them work doesn't merely cluster at harvest. I asked my father-in-law, who owns a farm in Kentucky, how the work is generally spread during the year. "In March and April," he said, "we work from sunrise to sunset preparing the soil: plowing, disking, then harrowing. Finally we plant, fertilizing at the same time.

"During the summer we rotate between several jobs. About every six weeks we take up a crop of hay and alfalfa. Periodically we have to cultivate (drag a hoelike instrument between the rows of seedlings that breaks up the clods and kills the weeds). We also spray for bugs. In May or June we harvest the winter wheat and then with no-till farming immediately plant soybeans.

"In the fall, after the intensive work of harvesting in late September or October, we carry the grain to the elevators. Then we carry animals to market. With the onset of winter, we maintain buildings and machinery, haul hay to the animals, repair fences. There is bookkeeping and financial arrangements and planning for the year ahead. We may even have some time to rest and hunt. At the end of winter and in early spring, we monitor the animals that are calving." Evidently a farmer's possibilities for payoff are inexhaustible.

Likewise, for us God provides rich opportunities in every season. If strong and healthy, we can work hard. In an emotional wilderness, we can seek God and grow in faith. We can, if unemployed, maintain the church or help paint a friend's house. Bedfast with sickness, we can read. Alone, we can pray and memorize Scripture. Business success affords us the freedom to contribute larger amounts to the kingdom of God, whereas a financial squeeze invites us to humble ourselves. The key to seizing such opportunities is to respond in the way God directs.

The rewards of one ordained response—perseverance—are unpredictable, but inevitable. If we persist, God will bring closure to the season. At the appointed time God will give the command, and the situation will reverse.

Peter, the Galilean fisherman, discovered that truth in his left-hand nets. One morning, after fishing unsuccessfully all night, Peter and his friends were preparing to quit.

On the shore stood Jesus. He called out, "Throw your net on the right side of the boat and you will find some." Imagine how ridiculous it seemed to these leathery fishermen to haul in the net, only to cast out the other side, a difference in location of maybe four feet!

Nevertheless, they threw the net one more time and quickly landed a school of fish. So great was the catch they could scarcely hoist it into the boat. What if they had knocked off work at 3:00 A.M.?

This story raises tantalizing possibilities. It shows that past futility is irrelevant. The future has as much potential for sudden change as the power of Christ's command. What miracle might we, by quitting, forfeit? No matter how hopeless the situation, we can persevere, knowing that a word from Jesus can fill our nets.

Wait for God to Change the Season

The third requirement for synchronizing with the season is that we patiently wait.

I asked Teri what made perseverance the most difficult during Rebekah's heart problems. "It was the waiting," she said, "not knowing. . . ."

After Rebekah's first surgery and the two-week ordeal of her recovery in the hospital, Vince and Teri brought her home to sleep once again in her own crib. Despite all the uncertainties, it was comforting to have her home. Compared to the trauma of her brush with death and the blow of surgery, she seemed markedly better, with every day bringing a small measure of improvement.

Nights were tough, though. For several months Rebekah's worst problem was not her heart. "She would be up all night coughing," says Teri, "choking and gagging, spitting up mucus. She also had terrible constipation problems and would just scream for hours."

They held on one day at a time. Months passed. Christmas came, and they enjoyed a special winter holiday with the girl they now called their miracle baby. For Christmas they gave her four rattles, and her grandmother gave her a Cabbage Patch doll.

With the coming of the new year, however, they noticed a haunting sign: a blue tint to her skin. They rushed her to the doctors, who summarily ordered another heart-catheterization procedure.

"Two hours long," said the cardiologist. Teri sat on a blue vinyl-covered chair in the waiting room, with other mothers of sick children nervously reading, smoking, and talking around her, while she read her Bible. "Every place I opened, the Bible talked about healing," Teri says. "I was getting so excited just imagining the doctors coming out and saying, 'There's nothing wrong with her.' I was sure of it."

There were no progress reports from nurses. Two hours passed. Three . . . then four. After five hours the cardiologist, still wearing his sterile green uniform with "Children's Memorial Hospital" stamped in small black letters on the shirt, finally came through the doors. Teri recalls, "His eyes were bloodshot. He looked terrible."

"It's bad news," he said.

Rebekah's repaired pulmonary veins were closing. As a result, her lungs had been harmed severely. "It's very danger-ous," said the surgeon. "She may have intrinsic lung disease." If that was the case, she would die. It would be irreversible.

They planned surgery; once again death stood in the shad-ows. They would try to reopen her pulmonary veins and—if she wasn't too weak—get a lung sample for testing. The doc-tors braced Vince and Teri for nothing but negative: Even if they could reopen the veins, they might close back up again; more critical, if the lung biopsy brought bad news, death was inevitable. This was the medicine of desperation.

For one week they awaited an opening in the surgical sched-ule. Finally it came, and Vince and Teri went home to pack a suitcase. While there, Teri opened her Scripture calendar to the next day's verse. February 22, 1985: "A new heart also will I give you, and a new spirit will I put within you: and I will take away the stony heart out of your flesh, and I will give you an heart of flesh" (Ezekiel 36:26 KJV).

Teri says, "I'm not into fortune cookies and all that stuff. But when we turned the calendar to that date . . . I just stood there crying. I started yelling to Vince, 'You gotta see this, you gotta see this.' The next day I taped that on her bed when she went into surgery because I knew those were God's com-forting words."

It would be a day of mixed emotions. In the operating room the surgeons successfully reamed Rebekah's pulmonary veins and also took the telltale lung biopsy. Knowing that her chest was once more neatly stitched closed over a tiny beating heart, however, offered Vince and Teri little relief. "Whether she came out alive," says Vince, "was not the key. It didn't mean it was a successful surgery. We had to wait for that lung bi-opsy. They had to send it out of state, and we had to wait almost a week to get the results. So it was a week of 'If it comes back negative, she's just going to die. And if it comes back positive, she's going to live . . . for now.' "

During that long, long week, despite spasms of panic—"While that lung biopsy is en route, you see her struggle; you see them put a chest tube into her, and all of a sudden your mind starts flip-flopping"—Vince and Teri experienced something miraculous: peace and hope.

"Even in moments of disappointment," says Teri, "there was a peace that would come over me. I didn't flip out or say, 'God, you lied to me.' Instead, in my heart would be, 'That's okay. God's just going to do it a different way, that's all.' This peace never let my faith be totally shaken. It was supernatural. Nervousness and worry come naturally for me, yet I didn't have to meditate for this peace or con myself into it. It wasn't like positive thinking. God just put it into me."

Teri's peace was justified. The biopsy report finally returned—negative. Eight months old, still weighing only eight pounds, brown-eyed Rebekah had, nevertheless, bounded over another huge hurdle.

*   *   *

Waiting, which feels so useless, is more spiritual than we think. Psalm 27:14 says, "Wait for the Lord; be strong and take heart and wait for the Lord." Sometimes waiting is "all" God wants us to do. But don't misconstrue waiting as inactivity, as hibernation. We don't crawl into a cave, curl up, and dormantly slumber until the advent of a season more to our liking. Rather we wait with active prayer, active faith, active anticipation, active Bible reading, active submission. True godly waiting energizes great spiritual vitality.

Not only is waiting more spiritual than we think, it is more productive than we imagine. Isaiah 64:4 says that God

". . . acts on behalf of those who wait for him." For patient men and women, God accomplishes more in a moment than man can do in a millennium. After we fulfill His purposes, He sovereignly ushers in another season.

Some will object, "I don't wait for anything; I make things happen." Like General Patton they claim to "find a way or make a way." "If it's not raining, send up a plane to seed the clouds."

That sounds impressive, but it overlooks one significant factor: the sovereign God. Few people have succeeded at hurrying the Lord. If He is wielding time as a tool, steadfast waiting remains our only recourse. In winter an impatient farmer would be less than prudent to drive his tractor through icy fields trying to thrust seeds into frozen soil. In summer he wouldn't roll his huge combine through the furrows to prematurely harvest three-inch seedlings. Neither can a Christian force spiritual seasons or fruit ahead of their time.

As they endured the pain of a long wait, Vince and Teri found that two things helped them overcome:

1. *Try to help others.* The natural tendency is to fixate on our own problems, but God wants to broaden our vision: "I really felt Him telling me," says Teri, "that every situation I was in was for the sake of other people. The Lord was concerned about everybody there, not just me and my troubles."

We often overlook how well our struggles equip us to help others. "Because of everything we went through, we could relate better to other people in the hospital," says Teri. "There were two opportunities a day to minister to others. I would talk with other families, pray for them, and try to lead them closer to the Lord. When I saw all the sorrow around me, I knew that was one of the reasons God had me there."

Looking outward instead of inward helps keep waiting in perspective. "There are so many reasons why God allows things," says Teri. "It's eternal, not just temporary. These all add up to eternal things."

2. *Remember what God has already done.* New crises often cause temporary amnesia. Although the Israelites, for example, had seen God deliver them out of Egypt by supernatural plagues and the miraculous parting of the Red Sea, each time they encountered a food or water shortage they still would panic and doubt God. They never learned from the past how to believe for the future.

Teri found that "at the times when Vince was down, I would be there to say, 'Remember when God did this.' Then another time I would be down, but he would be up and would remind me.

"We had to keep reminding ourselves what God had said. In February, when Rebekah was eight months old and things were such an ordeal, I found Psalm 42:5 where David said, 'Why are you downcast, O my soul? . . .' Then he says that he *remembered* God and how the Lord continually directs His love toward him. By the end of the psalm, he wasn't downcast anymore. When you think about what God has done in the past, you say, 'Yes, God is great. He did it then. He'll do it now.' "

*   *   *

But is waiting worthwhile? How do we know a season is coming that merits such patience?

Of course, everything in the Christian life rests on faith, and in this matter our faith rests in the assurance that God has a destiny for each of us. He foreknew us in the womb and has anointed us to fulfill a specific purpose, just as David of Bethlehem was anointed as a teenager to assume the throne of Israel years later. However, like David, we rarely reach our goal by a straight line, seldom by the shortest distance between two points. More often we walk a bewildering maze.

David's patience while walking the maze as a fugitive and his willingness to wait for God's ordained time to fulfill his destiny was remarkable, especially at two apparently opportune moments. To set the stage, recall first that, after he slew Goliath and became a military hero, David had to run for his life from jealous King Saul. For the next several years he crisscrossed the land of Palestine as Public Enemy Number One.

David's first opportunity to "find a way or make a way" came quite accidentally. Once, as he and his followers hid in a cave from Saul and his warriors, the king himself entered the cave alone to relieve himself. David and his men huddled only yards away. This was his chance, and the odds couldn't have been better. Nevertheless, David merely crawled up and cut off a piece of Saul's robe, obtaining evidence of his absence of hostility.

Confronted later with the fabric proof of David's loyalty, Saul softened momentarily, then resumed his jealous pursuit of David's scalp.

A second suitable moment arose. Months later, on another search-and-destroy mission, Saul's men pitched camp for the night with the king safely located in the center. In the middle of the night, however, David and his general crept into the camp. They edged by the dozing guards and walked right up to Saul, who was asleep with his spear stuck in the ground near his head. David's Green Beret companion whispered, "Today God has delivered your enemy into your hands. Now let me pin him to the ground with one thrust of my spear; I won't strike him twice" (1 Samuel 26:8).

This was it, David's window of opportunity. With the nod of his head he could move out of a chilling season into brighter and warmer days. He had waited long enough, many would say.

David replied, "Don't destroy him! Who can lay a hand on the Lord's anointed and be guiltless? As surely as the Lord lives, the Lord himself will strike him; either his time will come and he will die, or he will go into battle and perish. But the Lord forbid that I should lay a hand on the Lord's anointed . . ." (1 Samuel 26:9–11).

Here again, David expresses one of the rarest of traits: He was willing to wait for God, no matter how difficult his present affairs. He considered God's purpose worth persevering for. Eventually his confidence was rewarded, and his words were prophetic. Saul was indeed killed in battle. In short order, one of Israel's twelve tribes acclaimed David king. Then, seven years later, all Israel hailed him as their leader. Destiny fulfilled.

David's life illustrates well the adventure of synchronizing with the season. We find shimmering opportunity, but wilting hardship. Great potential, but terrifying risk. Glacier-slow progress, then sudden avalanching breakthroughs. Trouble, then triumph. At times David wondered whether God even remembered his name, yet centuries later Jesus Himself is called the Son of David. Equally impressive, in one New

Testament verse David is called "the man after the heart of God." Yes, summer finally did arrive.

The essential strength that brought David through all this tornado turbulence and uncertainty was perseverance. David clung to his God, weathered the storms, and found infinite blessings. If we will likewise persevere through the seasons ordained by God, we too have a green future.

6
To Exercise Faith

Midnight marathons can wreck your faith.

Cherrie, who lived in Colorado, was pregnant again. This was frightening news, since she had suffered several previous miscarriages. Nevertheless, she began praying and putting her trust in the Lord. Her mother, who had been attending church with her, was less composed. "Why would God allow this?" With her voice quivering and breaking with anxiety, she admitted to a church friend, "I don't think I can take this again. I don't know what I'll do if the baby dies." Clearly, with this pregnancy much was at stake.

Cherrie sought intensive care. She began seeing a specialist and asked her church to pray. They did, both for the pregnancy and for Cherrie's mom, who no longer attended services. For months Cherrie walked the edge, entering the hospital several times and finally becoming bedfast at home.

After eight months it ended. Cherrie delivered a healthy baby girl. There was, however, a miscarriage in this bittersweet story: mom's faith. Even after the healthy birth, she stayed far from God.

Crises tend to raise wooly questions. *Why does God allow*

this? Why doesn't God change things? At such perilous times we become serious theologians. *What do I really believe? Can I keep trusting the Scriptures with all this going on?* Unfortunately for some people, along the way faith may grow threadbare.

On the other hand, problems can firmly reinforce the fabric of faith. Those who respond with renewed trust in the Lord will find their faith multiplied.

One thing is sure: Our faith will never be the same. A perseverance situation pushes us one way or the other. Like a heavy load strapped to a man's back, it either strengthens the muscles or forces a collapse.

The better we understand the snug relationship between faith and perseverance, the stronger both will be. One analogy is especially helpful.

Cleated Faith

August 1985. At nineteen thousand feet on Mount Pik Pobedy in Asia, three American and twelve Soviet mountain climbers sit shivering in a tent. Outside a ferocious storm, which has raged for nearly two days, is burying them under three feet of snow. "Going down now," cautions one experienced climber, "risks near certain avalanche." Above, the four thousand vertical feet of ice and rocks separating them from the summit is now blanketed with an impassable snow cover. To climb, to descend, to stay—nowhere is safe.

Their plight hardly surprises them. They knew all too well about the six climbers killed on this mountain by an avalanche the previous year, and in excellent weather. On arrival they had even met a Soviet team bringing down bodies. Moreover, they knew the grim statistics: Over the years, 180 had conquered Pik Pobedy, while 45 had died. "At best," their senior trainer had predicted, "we have a 4 percent chance."

For several of the climbers the goal was honor. Conquering this mountain would qualify them for the title, bestowed by one mountain climbing society, of "Snow Leopard." So, despite the odds, they had ventured forth. And now they wait in their tents, wind howling, fingers freezing. "What do the Americans want to do?" asked a Soviet. What could they do, but wait. . . .

Then things started happening. As the storm finished, the wind blew so strongly it swept a path through the icy rocks. Triumphantly, one man shouted, "Our chances for the summit have improved to 5 percent." Mustering their strength, they set out for the top. At this point they were, because of oxygen deprivation, suffering high-altitude headaches, nausea, and vomiting. One team member was spitting bright red blood into the snow. They passed a frozen corpse sitting upright in a drift. No time for funerals.

Hours later, at 4:40 P.M., August 22, 1985, they stood at 24,406 feet above sea level—on the pinnacle of Pik Pobedy.

Those with cleated, persevering faith strikingly resemble these mountain climbers. Driven by our goals and needs, we are willing to suffer if necessary to reach the peak, knowing meanwhile that others have failed. Sometimes we are pinned down, progressing little and hazarding much. Nevertheless, despite the overwhelming odds, we keep climbing.

Different people scale various, treacherous paths. For example, men and women who are suffering affliction must persevere in the belief that God will deliver them. Those who minister for the Lord must persevere in the confidence that God will bless their work. People who are wrestling against doubts about Christianity must persevere in the assurance that God is there and He has spoken through His Son, Jesus. Those who feel tempted by sinful pleasures must persevere in the conviction that God rewards righteousness and judges wickedness. The common denominator: faith that overcomes.

This faith-climb hardly qualifies as sport. On the contrary, faith is serious business, for two critical reasons.

First, faith serves as the only foundation of our relationship with God. Without faith we don't have God: ". . . Anyone who comes to him must believe that he exists," says Hebrews 11:6, "and that he rewards those who earnestly seek him." Furthermore, the Gospel declares that we are saved by faith in Christ, not by our good works. ". . . The righteous," says Romans 1:17, "will live by faith." Faith is our ticket to the game—without faith, no seat and no standing room.

Second, our level of faith measures out how much God will bless us. Like the spigot on a faucet, it either allows a splashing stream of water or restricts the flow to a drip. For instance, when Jesus returned to His hometown of Nazareth to minister, His former neighbors, who had seen Him grow from infancy, had difficulty respecting His new stature and authority. The Bible remarks sadly that Jesus could not do many miracles there because of their unbelief. Their skepticism turned off the spigot on God's blessing. "According to your faith," said Jesus, "will it be done to you" (Matthew 9:29).

Faith never climbs solo. It is totally intertwined with perseverance. Roped together like two mountaineers, faith and perseverance climb as a team over every cliff and chasm, or slip and plummet as one.

Let's examine two strong loops of the knot that binds them.

Faith Motivates Perseverance

The relationship between faith and perseverance is as certain and predictable as the laws of physics. When science identifies a cause-and-effect relationship, that means one thing always, without fail, produces a certain effect. Boiling water produces steam, and fire, smoke. In the same manner, faith motivates perseverance.

True believers are tenacious, clinging like pitbulls to the object of their faith. The stockbroker who has painstakingly researched a company and concluded that their management team is first rate and their product quality high will not dump his shares three weeks after purchase just because their value tumbles for a few days. If anything, he'll buy more shares while the price is low, willing to invest even deeper because of his confidence in the company's future. He has clamped his teeth into a winner.

The key to such faith is spiritual, rather than natural, vision. "We walk by faith," says 2 Corinthians 5:7 (NKJV), "not by sight." Immediate circumstances are irrelevant for those with pitbull faith because God can reverse any situation, part any river, heal any sickness, solve any problem. No surprise, then, that faith can persevere indefinitely; 20/20 faith can do nothing else.

What a difference between good and bad vision. Nearsighted, short-term faith, which fizzles after setbacks or waffles under pressure, is shallow and perilously dependent on tangible evidence. It is shown to be faith, not in God, but in circumstances. Long-term, persevering faith, which has continued despite the lack of visible proof, is shown to be faith in God. It has stood the test of time.

Consider the faith of Ken Dignan.

"If you really have faith," said Ken's friends, "you'll take off your brace."

Only three months old in the Lord and totally dedicated to doing God's will, Ken, twenty, weighed their advice. Stricken by polio at age fourteen months, he had undergone four corrective surgeries on his arms and legs and had decided to keep walking despite severe curvature of the spine, a left leg thin and atrophied, and a weak left knee. If he misstepped even on a pebble, his leg would buckle. The thought of laying the brace aside was terrifying.

But if that was faith, he would do it. "God can heal anything," reasoned Ken, "even my body." One Sunday morning he took his leap of faith. He went to church without his metal support on, announcing to everyone, "I'm healed." Meanwhile, he could hardly walk. He was holding his breath and enduring excruciating pain.

Later, it happened. After church that night, as Ken stood in his kitchen talking to his parents, his left leg, which had been throbbing and trembling, twisted behind him. He felt a terrible crack, and, like a Tinkertoy splintering beneath a 150-pound weight, his emaciated leg collapsed. He veered to the tile floor and struck his head. While he lay writhing in pain, his leg swelled up like a balloon.

He spent the next three months in a leg cast. Anyone who had not grown up overcoming one setback after another would have had a heart as broken as Ken's tibia. Not Ken. "I wasn't mad at God," he said. "I just figured something went wrong. God hadn't told me to do what I did; I was just listening to my friends."

His friends were equally undaunted. "You can't give up,"

they said. "When you get the cast off, you're gonna have that healing. Don't put that brace back on."

"Cast-off day" finally arrived. The doctors sawed away the itchy plaster, and Ken decided to follow his buddies' advice: His brace stayed in the closet. For the next two weeks he hobbled around on a leg even more atrophied than before. "I didn't feel any lack of faith," says Ken. "I was just trying to help God heal me. My feeling was, 'If this is what I've got to do, I'll do it.' "

Gung-ho Ken set his eyes on the future. He traveled with his church youth group to investigate a college and limped unaided down the sidewalks of Minneapolis. That night, outside an ice-cream shop, standing with determination on two courageous legs, Ken once again heard that gruesome snap, and with his face contorted by pain he slammed to the pavement.

Ken has learned some concrete lessons about faith. He wears his brace now, eighteen years later. But make no mistake, his faith is stronger than ever, only better informed. "I never got mad at God. I just felt like, *Man, I'm missing the boat. It's not God, it's me and my friends who are botching things.* So I said, 'God you're probably doing something that we don't know anything about.' "

While recuperating, Ken sensed God's gentle teaching in his heart. "As I thought about it over those months, I felt the Lord saying, 'Just love Me. Something's happening that you don't understand. Don't try to force My hand. Don't try to heal yourself. Don't put Me in a box.' "

Ken also learned one vital principle from the Scriptures. "There are reasons why miracles may not happen to the extent you want. God told Paul that He wouldn't heal the thorn in his flesh but that Paul would be given extra grace (2 Corinthians 12:7–10). And I feel that is what God has told me. But that doesn't mean He won't heal me someday. I still receive prayer for healing—I've been anointed with enough oil to fill the ocean—and I know God will heal me someday, whether in this life or the age to come."

Full of faith despite facts, Ken reminds me of the men and women in the Who's Who list of the Bible. They had no idea what God was doing, but they trusted in Him nevertheless. David, for instance, whom the Bible describes as the man after the heart of God, plaintively prayed, *"How long*, O Lord? Will you forget me forever? *How long* will you hide your face from me? *How long* must I wrestle with my thoughts and every day have sorrow in my heart? *How long* will my enemy triumph over me? Look on me and answer, O Lord my God. Give light to my eyes, or I will sleep in death" (Psalm 13:1–3 italics added).

In other words, "Lord, I'm gonna die if you don't do something quick." Who hasn't felt this way? As a sign of His compassion, God has acknowledged our feelings by inspiring David's Psalm 13 prayer. And since David, the celebrated forefather of Jesus, felt this way, it isn't unusual that we will. To wonder "How long?" does not necessarily indicate a deficient walk with God.

Still, wondering "How long?" is no excuse for doubting. At the conclusion of his prayer David affirms, "But I trust in your unfailing love; my heart rejoices in your salvation." Never mind his agonized plea for haste, David still trusts in his God. Frustration and faith are not mutually exclusive. His faith wondered but didn't waffle, for the genuine article can do but one thing, persevere.

The cause: faith. The effect: perseverance. That is the first characteristic of the mountaineer's knot binding the two. The second characteristic is:

Perseverance Perfects Faith

Perseverance situations, I noted at the beginning of this chapter, can wreck faith. True, only if we respond wrongly. But with the proper biblical response, midnight marathons will train, augment, pump up, strengthen, buttress, fortify, and supernaturally perfect faith. God intends to vitalize our faith with nuclear force.

True faith reacts on the plutonium of challenge. Like a runner with pure speed who first cuts loose on the high school 440 track, or the artistically gifted girl who first picks up a charcoal pencil, believers sooner or later explode with confidence and excitement when trials threaten. At such times faith is in its element.

"Well, it sounds like I flunk that test," many will say. "My confidence takes a nosedive." If so, what can we do? Since our whole relationship with God depends on faith, and faith measures out God's blessings, what prospects do we have if ours is dwarfed by a mustard seed?

Thankfully, God offers remedial education. Instead of perpetually flunking us, He has designed a curriculum to strengthen our faith—even if we are as weak as kindergartners. If we will do our homework, anyone can graduate with a master's degree in faith. The program (described in terms of a physical education class) is outlined in Hebrews 12:1, 2:

> . . . Let us *run with perseverance*
> the race marked out for us.
> Let us fix our eyes on Jesus,

the author and perfecter of our faith.
who for the joy set before him
endured the cross. . . .

Note from this verse five principles about strengthening faith.

1. *Faith can grow.* Instead of being one of those either-you've-got-it-or-you-don't abilities, faith is perfectable. Any teachable Christian can someday exercise great faith. Just as the Lord molds our character—knowing full well how extensive a project that will be—so He trains our faith. To resign ourselves to permanent doubt would be like accepting as permanent the shortness of a newly planted redwood. Trees grow; faith grows.

2. *Jesus is determined to increase our faith.* Jesus, as the Author and Perfecter of our faith, travails more over its vitality than we do. We are not twisting His arm. He is carefully writing the book on our faith, mapping out the plot, polishing each chapter, editing a manuscript destined to be a masterpiece. When we request, as did the disciples, "Lord, increase our faith," we can be sure He will.

3. *He marks out a racecourse that will strengthen our faith.* This Scripture uses another enlightening analogy, running a race, and suggests that Jesus sits down with a map to plan each runner's course. At my college, the cross-country team ran on the golf course. For their meets they sank markers into the ground to guide runners through a designed circuit. Cutting inside one of the markers, which would shorten the distance, disqualified any competitor. For the Christian, Jesus,

too, marks out a faith-strengthening course, and if we attempt to shorten it, we disqualify ourselves from greater faith.

4. *Perseverance is the key to reaching the finish line of faith.* Faith is strengthened in the same manner as a runner's cardiovascular system. His capacity increases daily as he increasingly taxes his heart and lungs, conquering one more hill, finishing one more mile. Likewise, by exerting our faith day after day, straining up the hill of adversities overcome many times before, faith is not weakened, but strengthened. No one has a better cardiovascular system than a marathoner, or stronger faith than finish-line Christians.

Although all races have finish lines, not all are marathons. This book could foster a mammoth misconception—that answers to prayer are always delayed. Thankfully, God answers many prayers quickly, if not immediately, and a certain part of our faith is buoyed by such immediacy. But there is another dimension of faith that remains puny without perseverance. Therefore, Jesus always marks out a marathon in some facet of our lives.

5. *Jesus can sympathize with our perseverance struggles, so He knows how to strengthen our faith.* Jesus is no stranger to the struggle of perseverance, as Hebrews 12:2 says, He "endured the cross." Because He Himself has persevered, He is able to author our finish-line faith.

* * *

Dateline: Several thousand B.C., somewhere in the Middle East. God speaks to a man, a very elderly man, and commands him to become a shipbuilder. (Perhaps, afterward, the retired gentleman nailed a sign in his front yard: "NOAH'S ARKS.")

Noah was at least four hundred years old, and yet the Lord commissioned him to build a three-story ark longer than a football field, a veritable supertanker. Imagine how overwhelmed Noah felt. This was before power tools, lumberyards, ship engineering, and hydraulic cranes. He stood several lifetimes beyond retirement age, with the aches and weariness to prove it.

The project would require mammoth exertions of strength: to chop down hundreds of large trees, haul them to the job site, split and plane them into planks, manufacture nails, hoist thousands of huge beams and planks into place, climb countless times up and down crude scaffolding, hammer boards together, mix hundreds of gallons of thick black pitch, lift those heavy black buckets up the scaffolding, and then spread the tar inside and out.

Think of it. The difficulty of smearing that pitch over thousands of square feet of rough lumber would surpass that of painting one entire house a hundred times over. How did his hands and shoulders and legs feel each night? How tough was it for him to roll out of bed in the morning? The scale and scope of this project defies modern imagination.

The construction of the ark by Noah and his sons ranks with the most phenomenal human feats of all time. It is perhaps the greatest feat of perseverance. Over the years required to complete it, Noah must have struggled repeatedly about whether to continue. No doubt passersby mocked him endlessly. Who had ever heard of a flood that would cover the world? Were the sore muscles and exhaustion and ridicule and expense and time and trouble worth it?

What could possibly lift Noah's perseverance to such superhuman levels? Hebrews 11:7 unveils his secret: "By faith Noah . . . built an ark to save his family." Had Noah doubted God's flood warning, he would have quit. Unsinkable faith powered his perseverance.

Faith and perseverance—knotted together like mountaineers, they rise in unison.

With all the risk and hardship, why do mountain climbers do it anyway? If they yearned simply to stand on the summit, helicopters, parachutes, or custom snowmobiles could more easily transport them. Clearly, the climb is the heart and soul of the venture.

In the same way, God could by His mighty hand whisk us to our destination, bypassing all the pain. But He values the climb: how we respond, how we grow, how we bond more deeply with Him. After we have reached the summit, what will burn indelibly in our hearts is the memory of our breathtaking ascent. As one man told me, "I wouldn't ever want to go through it again, but it was the most meaningful experience of my life. At the time, it was terrible and scary and overwhelming; but I look back on it now and see all the good that came out of it. It was worth it."

7
To Express Humility

At many times in our lives nothing short of a breakthrough will do. Jay and Rita were at that point. He had been in total command of his life, including running a New York company of his own. As a computer consultant he worked long hours and earned a solid income. Yet he and his new wife also found time for involvement in an embryonic church, she as secretary, he as a teacher. Both in their thirties, they were moving into an enriching new chapter in their lives.

Trouble came thick and fast. A disgruntled associate accused Jay of a business impropriety, which he denied out of hand, but the rumor spread to his clients and shortly he was out of business, plundered of what he valued more than money, his reputation. Inevitably, the stress imploded into his body. After experiencing some frightening symptoms—memory loss and incoherence—he visited the doctor, who discovered a crimped blood vessel in his head triggering the symptoms of a stroke without permanent harm. The cure was total rest.

He convalesced for several months. Afterward, intending to

start over, they moved into a new apartment in the suburbs.

Even with the new surroundings, they felt bankrupt in many ways. Financially, they were in ruins as weeks passed with Jay unable to find work. In their kitchen the cupboards were bare. Spiritually, their faith was traumatized. They couldn't understand how God could allow this, and Jay felt lingering resentment toward many, including the Lord. As a result, they had avoided church services for over six months. On his own, Jay continued to push buttons and pull levers, but no amount of strength, willpower, or savvy could budge his life off dead stop.

At such times, only a breakthrough will do. Troubled times resemble an expressway during rush hour where an accident has closed all traffic lanes. With cars on the left and right, in front and behind, the only hope is a tow truck to clear away the wreckage. Only the authorities can unlock gridlock.

Similarly, for whatever reason—sickness, unemployment, debt, depression—on some occasions only an act of God can free us. We realize how weak and limited is the arm of flesh, how utterly dependent we are on the almighty God for deliverance, breakthrough, success. The question then becomes, do we merely wait, or is there some response that God is seeking before He radios the tow trucks?

Humility Can Prompt Divine Breakthroughs

It is no secret whom God helps:

> . . . God opposes the proud
> but gives grace to the humble.

Humble yourselves, therefore,
under God's mighty hand,
that he may lift you up
in due time.

1 Peter 5:5, 6

God blesses the humble with breakthroughs. Five principles from these verses show how and why.

1. *God gives grace.* Grace is better than Christmas. *Grace,* God's broad smile upon us, is a rich biblical word that sums up everything the Lord freely gives, including blessings, love, salvation, mercy, healing, fruitfulness, success, wisdom, help, and joy. In a more narrow theological sense, grace means unmerited favor, undeserved blessing, gratuitous love. For instance, a friend of mine was recently hired for a new job one week before Christmas; nevertheless, his boss paid him the same Christmas bonus as full-year employees. Grace means God is no grinch.

Gridlock victims need grace. We can't earn the Lord's help. Moreover, we often have mapped out our own troubles through sin, foolishness, or misjudgments. Because we ignore God's scriptural directions, we don't deserve help. Yet—amazingly—God gives grace to the humble whether worthy or not. That's the definition of grace.

A notable example is Ahab, a peerless Old Testament scoundrel. Husband of the infamous and sleazy Jezebel and king of backslidden Israel, he lowered corruption and idolatry to new depths. Scripture says, "There was never a man like Ahab, who sold himself to do evil in the eyes of the Lord . . ." (1 Kings 21:25). After one particularly slimy transaction—the murder of a man because he wouldn't sell him his vineyard—God pronounced acid-strong judgment.

Ahab's response was astonishing. "He tore his clothes, put on sackcloth, fasted and walked meekly." In other words, he humbled himself before God. Even more remarkable is God's response, spoken to Elijah the prophet, "Have you noticed how Ahab has humbled himself before me? *Because he has humbled himself,* I will not bring this disaster in his day, but I will bring it on his house in the days of his son" (1 Kings 21:29). Clearly, even if we have strayed afar, God responds to our sincere humility with abundant grace.

2. *God opposes the proud.* Breakthrough grace is withheld from them. What does ego have to do with gridlock? Either cause or effect:

First, self-exaltation may have caused our current troubles. Scripture warns, "He who exalts himself will be humbled."

One egomaniac learned this in dramatic fashion. A matchless builder and conquerer, he ruled as the most powerful king on earth. It went to his head, though, so after both a warning and a year's delay, God judged him. Insanity struck, and he joined the wild kingdom. He crawled in the fields, his nails growing into talons, his hair hanging in clumps, his mouth chewing grass.

Eventually the Lord healed his mind, and having learned his lesson, the king spoke these humble words, "Now I, Nebuchadnezzar, praise and exalt and glorify the King of heaven, because everything he does is right and all his ways are just. And those who walk in pride he is able to humble" (Daniel 4:37). The King of kings then graciously restored the king of Babylon to his throne.

Second, the fleshly reaction to gridlock is an ego surge. We resent failure, frustration, and helplessness. Our self-image takes a beating, and we may compensate by trying to exalt ourselves—the polar opposite of what will bring God's help.

3. *We must humble ourselves.* A few years of insanity won't suffice. As Nebuchadnezzar illustrates, although God will Himself humble our pride, we also must humble ourselves. Many respond defiantly, hardening their hearts and refusing to bow. However, if we confess sins and admit dependence on God, we will, at the proper time, receive a breakthrough.

Jay and Rita, who had suffered so many financial and physical difficulties, in the process wavering somewhat in faith, finally hit bottom; they knew they needed God's help. One Sunday morning they attended a new church. After a few weeks they went again, and on their third visit they did it: When opportunity was given for special prayer, they got up from their seats and walked to the front. To acknowledge such need in public is like dying.

Nevertheless, death, as an exalted seed illustrates, precedes life. Seeds are nurtured in the flower, the glory of the plant. From there the only way to fulfill their purpose is to dry out, fall to the ground, and disappear into the dirt. Until it dies, a seed remains sterile. But death isn't the end of the story.

4. *God lifts up the humble.* Once in the ground the seed begins the miracle of germination. First a tiny root grows. Then the stem presses upward, breaks through the clods, stretches its leaves toward the sky, and in the brightness of the sun blooms colorful flowers of its own. Its roots, nevertheless, cling in the dirt, still in humility. Through death and humility the seed finds glory.

Even so, God exalts those who humble themselves, unleashing grace and favor, bestowing miracles and blessings and breakthroughs.

Jay, who had humbled himself by coming forward for prayer, was looking for any work at this point, but his first love was urban planning, a field in which he had both a degree and much experience. One day, about two months after praying in church, Jay attended a seminar. He met a man associated with an agency that, coincidentally, had just lost its director. The necessary profile of education and experience matched Jay precisely. Within weeks he was in a new office, in his chosen field.

Humility is divinely powerful. Given God's promise to lift up the humble, the act of self-humiliation resembles the path of a ski jumper who leaps onto the downward slope, only to be hurled at the bottom of his descent into flight. Our slide gathers heavenly force for takeoff.

"He who humbles himself will be exalted," taught Jesus. His own life modeled—to the ultimate—this principle. He willingly "made himself nothing . . . ," says Philippians 2:7, 8, ". . . he humbled himself and became obedient to death. . . ." The very Son of God, from eternity honored in God's presence, chose while on earth to lower Himself for our sake. The recoil transcended the universe: "Therefore God exalted him to the highest place . . ." (Philippians 2:9).

We have a choice. Exalt ourselves, jump in the air, and gravity will bring us crashing to the ground. Humble ourselves, and God will grant grace, the force that propels us heavenward.

5. *We must persevere in humility until "due time."* God is the timekeeper, as Psalm 31:15 says, "My times are in your hands. . . ." Although God promises to lift us up, He doesn't

specify when: "Humble yourselves, therefore, under God's mighty hand," says 1 Peter 5:6, "that he may lift you up in due time." (Note: The words *due time* are translated from the Greek word *kairos*, "season.") The Lord alone knows the propitious time, not us. Accordingly, if we fail to persevere in humility, we sabotage the upturn planned by God.

Due-time elevation can surprise us; ask Moses. Recall that after his mid-life-crisis effort to bring justice to his people, Pharaoh chased him into the desert. Just as the seed nurtured in the flower must nestle into the soil, so Moses fell from the royal house of Egypt to the dry sticks of the Sinai outback. At age forty, when most people cash in on their dues, Moses lost everything.

Thereafter, humility came naturally, for he had much to be humble about. In his new career path he trailed sheep. He spent his days alone, save the company of his wooly charges, the wind, and the sand. Four decades of that affected him profoundly, as God affirmed years later, "Moses was a very humble man, more humble than anyone else on the face of the earth" (Numbers 12:3).

The Lord never lost track of Moses. One day, *in due time*, as Moses walked the sheep, a brightness caught his attention. He turned aside to examine, found a burning bush, and had what we would call, understatedly, a breakthrough: In a face-to-face with the Angel of the Lord, he received the most important mission imaginable, the deliverance of the Israelites from Egypt. Due time, for Moses, was forty years.

Yet it was time well spent. With God as timekeeper, due time was good time. Forty years of humiliation were hardly easy, but they prepared Moses for true breakthroughs.

There is a huge difference between a human turnaround and a divine breakthrough. Even without humbly serving

God, people can enjoy little upturns. But such progress is merely human, finite, temporary, meaningless relief. On the other hand, when we humble ourselves under God's mighty hand, we receive a breakthrough with eternal significance. With all of time and humanity in view, God wisely fits us into the puzzle in a manner that benefits us—and others—the most. In His love He arranges our destiny to bring us—and others—the greatest lasting happiness. Heaven-sent breakthroughs reflect an eternal scope and a universal dimension worthy of our infinite Lord and possible only through Him.

God's plans dwarf ours. On our own, and with such miniscule perspective, we map out great master plans for ourselves, which from God's viewpoint resemble a tricycle ride around the block. God, however, has laid out a world tour, a grand and noble destiny. So He graciously allows gridlock to bar us from puny, petty neighborhood trips. Until humility is complete, though, the plan is in park.

It is no coincidence that Moses, the most humble man on earth, became one of God's most exalted servants. The more faithfully we humble ourselves, the more forcefully grace propels upward. It is a law of spiritual physics: What goes down, of its own accord, must come up, much farther up than before. Moses began as somebody in Egypt; he finished as *somebody* before God.

Perseverance Is an Essential Expression of Humility

Given that humility causes breakthroughs, how do we express it? One prestigious annual event gives a clue.

The place: the congressional house chambers. The occasion: the president's State of the Union address. The room is packed with dark-suited men and women, the most powerful people in America: senators, congressmen, Supreme Court justices, cabinet officers, generals. Everyone is in place— except for one man. All these influential men and women, accustomed to having staffers, lobbyists, and journalists wait on them, are now waiting for the greatest man in government—the president of the United States. Finally the doors open and he strides down the center aisle, friends and foes alike paying their respects.

This scene illustrates the first of two critical principles about expressing humility:

1. *The lesser waits for the greater.* The president doesn't ar- rive first, standing at the podium saying hello as others en- ter. In England the queen doesn't step into her limousine and then sit until the chauffeur finishes his coffee break. At the hospital the doctor doesn't pace in the examination room, waiting for the patient to arrive. Generally we wait for the one in authority.

God being the King of kings, and we His subject creation, how fitting that we wait for Him. Moses, for example, waited on top of Mount Sinai for seven days until God beckoned him in to receive the tablets of stone. Only the humble can wait patiently, contritely for God's mighty deeds. Through perse- verance, therefore, we express and prove our humility.

The arrogant can't wait. They sense intuitively the chro- nological blow to their ego. For instance, several weeks ago I went to the bank with a deposit. In the lobby, they separate patrons into two lines, one for personal accounts and another for commercial. On Saturdays, with larger crowds, the tellers regularly ask those queued in long lines to walk over to the commercial windows. I had come, though, on Tuesday. The personal account line stretched long, so I brazenly strolled over to commercial accounts, where only one person was waiting. When my turn came, the clerk twenty feet away asked, "Are you here for a commercial transaction?"

She smelled a rat. I said, "No."

She pointed firmly to the personal accounts line and said, "You'll have to wait over there."

Trespassers get angry when caught. My momentary impulse was to walk into somebody's office and complain. *Do you think you have customers,* I thought, *with nothing better to do than wait in line while petty clerks stand there doing nothing?* Holding, nevertheless, to my outward calm, I turned from the commercial line, bypassed the other, and walked out the door.

It didn't take me long to recognize that my ego had taken over, and to thank God I hadn't made a greater fool of myself. The point here is that my bruised ego wouldn't let me wait. Pride erodes perseverance.

This helps explain some difficult-to-understand Bible stories. Have you ever wondered why God dealt so severely with the Israelites after the Exodus when they grumbled about lacking food and water? Recall that on one occasion grumbling resulted in a plague that killed twenty-three thousand. We read the story and think, *Three days in the desert without food and water would be pretty tough. It's not surprising they were a bit testy.*

Let's look at it from another perspective. They had already seen God's power and miracles: the plagues on Egypt and the parting of the Red Sea. They knew God could supply their need, so why not simply ask Him? Praying patiently was the logical thing to do. But it was also the humble thing, and so they didn't. They wouldn't submit to God and His timetable, and thus pride spawned complaints. Only the humble can pray, wait on someone greater, and persevere.

Setting the schedule is a control issue, therefore an ego issue. It is the sergeant who decides when the privates hear reveille. It is the president who sets office hours, not the secretary. Therefore, the proud demand control, that God do things upon request, not at His discretion. Humility demands that we unhand the timetable, relinquish control, and persevere.

The second critical principle about expressing humility is:

2. *The lesser must obey the greater.* When someone in authority commands us to do something and keep doing it, perseverance becomes an act of obedience. To give up is to go AWOL. A soldier who abandons his watch has broken orders and is liable to court-martial. The Christian who humbly acknowledges God's authority also recognizes the obligation to persevere in whatever God commands.

The prophet Elijah almost went AWOL. Because wickedness prospered in the land, he announced to Israel's wicked king, "As the Lord, the God of Israel, lives, whom I serve, there will be neither dew nor rain in the next few years except at my word" (1 Kings 17:1). At God's direction he ran and for several years laid low, first in a wilderness ravine and afterward with a poor widow.

The Lord then told Elijah to confront the king. In the subsequent showdown between the king's 850 false prophets and Elijah, God sent down fire from heaven to prove Himself and vindicate Elijah, who had the wicked prophets hastened by sword into eternity. So far everything was copacetic.

For a few brief hours Elijah was feeling pretty good. Then Jezebel, wife of the wicked king and chief patron of the decedents, threatened to retaliate. Elijah came unglued. He hightailed it south about sixty miles into the desert below the toe of the Mediterranean Sea.

He paused from his panic-stricken retreat to lie down beneath a straggly, weatherbeaten broom tree. For three and a half years he had endured wilting hardship and deprivation for the sake of his God. He had been willing to die in a duel with the bad guys. Finally he had thought his faithfulness and sacrifice would be rewarded—then Jezebel puts out a contract on him. Hit men would be combing the countryside. No place would be safe from the mob.

He just couldn't take it anymore. Slumped under the broom tree he prayed, "I have had enough, Lord. Take my life; I am no better than my ancestors." Elijah, a man of courage, determination, devotion, and zeal, was committing intercessory suicide.

God didn't oblige. After Elijah napped, an angel woke him, fed him, and sent him to the mountain of God. Following the forty-day journey there, he entered a cave. God asked him, "What are you doing here, Elijah?"

Still enormously defeated, he replied, "I have been very zealous for the Lord God Almighty. The Israelites have rejected your covenant, broken down your altars, and put your prophets to death with the sword. I am the only one left, and now they are trying to kill me too" (1 Kings 19:10). Elijah had every reason, obviously well rehearsed, to quit. His ministry was failing. No one cared for him. His future was worthless and frightening. Why go on?

God's response will surprise many. He didn't comfort or console. He didn't tell Elijah to experience the full depths of his emotion. He simply said, "Go back the way you came," and outlined a three-part mission: anoint two new kings and one new prophet.

What would Elijah do? He didn't feel like persevering. But Someone in authority, the Ultimate Authority, had commanded him to continue his calling. Now he must choose: humble himself and keep obeying, or rebel and quit.

Elijah stepped back into the ranks. He left the mountain of God and went to anoint the prophet. He persevered because he was following orders, because when push came to shove, he wouldn't think of doing other than God's will.

Our choice is no less dramatic. Admittedly, God will speak to few on Mount Horeb, yet He has spoken unmistakably in His Scriptures. He tells us to stand firm, give ourselves fully to the work of the Lord, love our enemies, keep believing, go the extra mile, pray, and not give up. The question is, will we humble ourselves and obediently persevere?

If so, like Elijah, we will follow the cycle of the seed. After his triumph over the 850 false prophets, Elijah was in the glory of the flower. But once Jezebel snarled her threats—and later God commanded him to persevere—he again faced the prospect of falling to the ground, nestling into the soil, and dying to self. And die he did.

The seed flowered. Elijah accomplished God's purposes, and one day a flaming chariot pulled by horses of fire appeared in the sky. It swooped down, picked up Elijah, and swept him deathless into heaven's majesty.

Apparently God thinks rather highly of those who humbly persevere.

8
To Receive Rewards

Large rewards make even the longest, toughest job easier. Clarence Berry was a California farmer. Normally in Fresno that's a thriving business, but hard times were wringing the life from his enterprise. Finally he had to sell out.

Later, in desperation he decided to travel north to the Yukon of Canada where gold had been discovered. Panning the frigid rivers, some prospectors had found today's equivalent of sixty-five dollars in a single dip. Lured by the hope of financial relief, but penniless, Berry borrowed money at exorbitant interest to purchase his travel ticket and prospecting gear. This venture would either rescue or bury him.

Once in Canada, he met his first great obstacle. The most direct way to penetrate the mountains that form a barrier to the hinterland was through a narrow breach called the Chilkoot Pass. Although direct, it was dauntingly difficult. After a four-mile trek up the foothills, prospectors leaned into a thousand-foot climb up a thirty-five-degree slope. The trail was strewn with immense boulders caked most of the year with solid ice. In winter, snow fell almost continually, reaching a depth of seventy feet. After scaling the pass, a prospector still had to raft hundreds of miles to the goldfields.

Berry began his odyssey with forty men. Together they trudged up the trail and eventually breached Chilkoot, but then a howling blizzard struck. It destroyed their supplies and buried the courage of thirty-eight of the men, who promptly turned back. With little more than the clothes on his back, Berry, a huge man with rocky biceps and massive shoulders, pressed on. Somehow he and his partner reached the goldrush town of Fortymile.

The easy part was over; now he had to find gold. He set out to prospect, panning the icy streams, digging in the permafrost, competing with fortune hunters, avoiding conmen. After years of slim payoffs, he finally took a job in Fortymile to keep food on the table. Who would have thought that there in town he could get his best lead?

*　　*　　*

The pursuit of rewards is a common motivation not only to fortune hunters, like Clarence Berry, but also to persevering Christians. God has ignited in each of us the burning hope that our good deeds will be rewarded, that there is eternal benefit in doing God's will. Especially as we endure what seem like incurable troubles—a turbulent marriage, an infirm loved one, daily migraines, a muleheaded colleague—we yearn to know whether there is some happy return for such unremitting hardship. Is there gold buried in this cold, forbidding life?

Meanwhile, we may twinge with guilt over such thinking. Is it selfish to want rewards? Is it unworthy of a Christian, somehow mercenary or greedy?

Apparently not, in the eyes of the Lord. On the contrary, Jesus encourages those suffering persecution with this hope, "Rejoice and be glad, because great is your reward in heaven" (Matthew 5:12). Moreover, in the Sermon on the Mount He *commands* His followers to lay up treasures in heaven. From beginning to end, the Bible offers future heavenly rewards as motivation for painstaking obedience. Plainly, the Lord does not regard our interest in rewards as a base desire.

Well then, that raises some questions. What rewards does God promise the persevering? Will they be worth the trouble? Why don't I see any rewards yet?

These questions are answered by five hope-inspiring, scriptural principles.

God's Rewards Beat Worldly Perks

Earthly rewards are gratifying, but vulnerable. Jan Stephenson, a professional golfer, was looking forward to an enjoyable evening with her husband at a Phoenix Suns' basketball game as guests of the owner. After dressing, she slipped on her Rolex watch, worth one thousand dollars, and a sapphire pendant, a prize from a tournament in Japan.

Later they pulled into the parking lot outside the stadium. Jan opened her door and stepped out of the car. Suddenly a man grabbed her, ripped off her watch, snatched her purse and pendant, and wrenched her wedding band from her finger. Before her husband could help, the mugger had fled. The thief did leave her with something: a splintered ring finger that required surgical screws and pins to repair.

The problem with this world's perks is they are diluted, or embittered, by sorrow. All are liable to loss, theft, corrosion, accident, disaster, and, therefore, cause anxiety. All prick the envy, coveting, and criticism of others, thereby souring once-happy relationships. All depend on our unhindered ability to enjoy, easily handicapped by sickness, tragedy, or depression.

Worst of all, at death we lose the benefit of earthly rewards forever.

God's rewards, on the other hand, generate pure satisfaction. Three characteristics reveal why.

SECURITY Neither burglars, inflation, nor market fluctuations can pierce the thick wall of safety that surrounds heavenly premiums, rendering such things as electronic surveillance systems, insurance, and steel safes unnecessary. Jesus said, "Store up for yourselves treasures in heaven . . . where thieves do not break in and steal" (Matthew 6:20).

LONGEVITY God's blessings outlast this world's "lifelong" investments. What most people consider their greatest prize, a home, becomes in only a few decades a handyman's burden, and eventually a bulldozer's dinner. Heavenly rewards, however, endure forever—indestructible and incorruptible. "Store up for yourselves treasures in heaven, where moth and rust do not destroy. . . ."

PLEASURE Bittersweetness will be no more. God's rewards will inspire undiluted happiness, untainted joy, pure delight, absolute enjoyment. "My people," says the Lord, "will receive a double portion and . . . they will rejoice in their inheritance; and so they will inherit a double portion in their land, and everlasting joy will be theirs" (Isaiah 61:7).

What exactly will these rewards be? A gold watch to monitor eternity? Scripture offers only a veiled, often symbolized, peek. More than likely many things regarded as priceless in this age will be insignificant in our glorified state, and what will be treasured then we scarcely understand or appreciate now. Nevertheless, we can clearly conclude three inviting things about the content of our rewards:

1. *The Lord will reward us with treasures.* Jesus invited us to stockpile "treasures in heaven." Hence, whatever we receive will be lavishly valuable, the equivalent of gold, jewels, money, and treasures here on earth. Like Solomon in his heyday, many will be wealthy and prosperous.

2. *The Lord will reward us with honor.* God, alone worthy of glory, will nonetheless highly honor before all heaven's hosts those who have done His will. "There will be . . . glory, honor and peace," says Romans 2:9, 10, "for everyone who does good. . . ." "These have come so that your faith . . . may be proved genuine," 1 Peter 1:7 affirms, "and may result in praise, glory and honor when Jesus Christ is revealed." God-given honor will make the fame and celebrity of this world seem like a tar and feathering.

3. *The Lord will reward us with the inheritance.* The gist of this big subject: Just as the child of a wealthy landowner inherits all his parents' possessions, so we as God's adopted children will inherit the farm universal. First Corinthians 3:21–23 says, ". . . All things are yours, whether Paul or Apollos or Cephas or the world or life or death or the present or the future—all are yours, and you are of Christ, and Christ is of God." This includes delegated authority: "To him who overcomes," said Jesus in Revelation 3:21, "I will give the right to sit with me on my throne"; and full citizenship in God's government with all the blessings that entails: "Has not God chosen those . . . to inherit *the kingdom* he promised those who love him?" (James 2:5). All things considered, most saints will rather enjoy eternity.

God's generosity soars above even our wildest dreams like a home run over a pitcher's head. On one recent winter day as we rode in the car, my sons, Aaron and Ben, were discussing baseball cards. José Canseco, Don Mattingly, Ken Griffey, Jr., hot prospects, rookies, MVPs. . . . Of one player Aaron said, "Dad, I read in my magazine that last year he got paid forty thousand dollars for every home run he hit." I was impressed. He was certainly playing in a different financial league than most humans. But not in a different league regarding ultimate rewards. According to the Scriptures just surveyed, for every righteous deed of ours, God's reward will put to shame even the biggest baseball bonus.

Knowing that can make all the difference. With but a rough sketch of God's heavenly rewards, one thing is clear: They are worthy of supreme sacrifice. If we keep these future blessings in view, motivation will be the least of our problems.

Of course, common sense tells us that God doesn't reward arbitrarily. In order to qualify, what must we do, and how must we do it?

God Rewards Anything Done for Him

God has exacting standards for what merits rewards. By far the weightiest factor is our motives: Why are we doing this? For whom, ourselves or the Lord? No matter the size or scope of the action, God rewards anything done for Him.

The Judge of all the earth, who monitors even sparrows and the hairs on our head, will carefully and meticulously lavish blessings on us for even the smallest righteous deed. A mere cup of water for the thirsty, said Jesus, will not go unnoticed. A secret prayer, He assured us, expressed to please God rather than men, will not be forgotten. If our Father repays these tiny devotions with heaping heavenly treasures, how much more the agonizing trials of perseverance, maintained for His sake alone.

Our overtaxed emotions, however, say no. While persevering we don't generally feel as though we're accomplishing much, or even doing good. Mostly because perseverance lacks closure. Often we can't point to something and say, "Here's what I did." Instead, we might say, "Lord, here's what I tried to do." In effect, then, perseverance feels like failure in process, almost like shameful activity. Without that clear-cut finish, that terminus, that ribbon on the package, we feel like underachievers bringing home a bad report card.

Job knew the feeling, having borne in full measure the semi-shame of perseverance. In the process, he learned something surprising about what God rewards. Job's bad day began with him as the wealthiest man of the land, owner of thousands upon thousands of sheep, camels, oxen, and donkeys. In addition he boasted many servants. The joy of his life, though, were his seven sons and three daughters. Suddenly, without warning, the first rumble of an avalanche sounded in the hurried footsteps of a servant, who announced that land pirates had pilfered his oxen and donkeys and murdered many servants.

Then it seemed the whole mountain tumbled down upon him. Additional messengers reported the loss of his sheep, camels, servants—and ten precious children! Plundered of all but his health, wife, and land, he plunged into mourning, victim of total catastrophe.

Not quite. Soon he broke out in oozing skin ulcers from head to toe. Hemorrhaging emotionally, he sat down in a pile of ashes and resigned himself to scraping, with a piece of broken pottery, the mucous crust from his sores.

The avalanche finished with a hailstorm of small stones.

Bystanders tormented him. His wife urged him to sin by speaking against God. His friends pronounced these troubles his own fault. Even a brash youth pilloried Job as guilty. It was slow death by a thousand cuts, from all directions, in all ways. Seated in the dustheap, still a righteous man, haunted by his past, tortured by the present, terrified by the future, what meritorious thing did Job do?

Seemingly nothing. He didn't utter any noble prayers. He didn't divy up his property for the poor. All he did was stubbornly refuse to turn against God. His most laudable deed appears to have been a nondeed.

Eventually God entered the scene, and He wasn't happy, at least with Job's onlookers. He promptly set the records straight. First He made it plain that His reasons for allowing Job's suffering were as unsearchable as His infinite wisdom and power. Then He vindicated Job before his accusers. Finally He gladly reversed Job's lot, prospering him once again in every way—twofold. He gave him twice as many sheep, camels, oxen, and donkeys. He duplicated his family, seven sons and three daughters. In the end, all Job's friends and acquaintances came to comfort him with gifts of gold and silver, and he lived one hundred forty *more* years. Ah, sweet justice.

In all this the Lord is plainly rewarding Job for something, but for what? What deed? What righteousness? Simply this: perseverance. The Bible devotes one entire book to the story of a man who did *nothing more* than persevere, and in the capstone chapter God rewarded him exorbitantly. In God's eyes, perseverance ranks as one of the greatest of all good deeds, and worthy of the richest rewards.

How can something that feels so fruitless be so deserving? The answer must be that God views decisions as deeds.

Heaven records ongoing perseverance as hundreds, even thousands, of good decision-deeds, with every moment-by-moment choice to endure being pleasing to the Lord. Each decision, each extra minute, is etched in God's book and will be celebrated at Judgment Day.

The indispensable key, though, is to persevere for the right reason, ". . . for the Lord, not for men, since you know that you will receive an inheritance from the Lord as a reward . . ." (Colossians 3:23, 24).

Most of God's Rewards Are Delayed

Pay your workers while the sweat is wet on their brows. So goes one maxim about motivating employees; one that doesn't seem to have made a strong impression on the Lord. Even His most faithful, dedicated workers can see meager results, unusual hardship, deep frustration, and harsh criticism for long durations. Why so?

In reality, only to the naked eye do God's servants labor unrewarded. The spiritual eye sees otherwise, that the Lord showers us with immediate spiritual blessings—far more enriching to the soul—for all our righteous acts. In addition, with spiritual vision we see that the bulk of our visible rewards are simply delayed until the final judgment.

If our faith rests solely on here-and-now dividends, we will be quickly disillusioned. The heroes of the Bible had no such misconceptions. In his ministry, Paul the apostle said he felt like "the scum of the earth" (1 Corinthians 4:13), having spent years in jails and suffered hardship upon hardship for decades. With complete frankness he said, "If only for this life we have hope in Christ, we are to be pitied more than all men" (1 Corinthians 15:19). In other words, if the visible

111

rewards already received were all he was getting, it wasn't worth it. Had he expected to see all his rewards in this age, Paul would have quit on the quick.

You see, Paul was no dupe. He invested his life as logically as any hard-nosed businessmen, who also live quite happily with delayed rewards. Tucked away in thousands of safe-deposit boxes are pieces of 100 percent cotton-bond paper bordered with intricate green patterns. The text, large print and small, promises to pay at a later date a sum of money. An investor buys this bond for, say, $1,000, and ten years later at 10 percent compounded daily he receives back $2,717.90. Delayed rewards, the fundamental principle of accumulating wealth, aren't so bad after all.

Some bonds mature in just six months. Although we will receive our weightiest rewards at the final judgment, God does bestow some rewards in the present. Jesus said, "No one who has left home or brothers or sisters or mother or father or children or fields for me and the gospel will fail to receive a hundred times as much *in this present age* . . ." (Mark 10:29, 30 italics added). However that is fulfilled, notice the present-age time frame. Jesus hardly excludes earthly rewards.

Ken Dignan, the victim of polio at fourteen months, understands well the relationship between perseverance and present blessings. Unabashed by his twice-broken leg, Ken decided to attend bible college, where he faced a new challenge: high mobility. Because of his severe curvature of the spine, deformed right arm, and withered left leg, the campus presented a daily obstacle course. "I can't climb stairs, get up higher curbs, or get out of a chair without assistance," says Ken. "This was before the days of ramps and special curbs for the handicapped. Usually someone would push me over in a wheelchair, but sometimes I walked. After half a block I would have to pause and recoup my strength, then go on. Sometimes I fell. At the curbs I would have to get kind of a running start and then hope my foot would hit the top."

Although Ken never doubted that he would graduate, he did worry about finding a wife. For years he didn't have a date. In his senior year, however, he met Joni. "The biggest turning point for me personally was meeting somebody who took the time to get to know me." As Ken's final year in school wound down, their relationship grew. In the spring he graduated with highest honors, including being the valedictorian of his class. One year later they married.

Still he wasn't satisfied. Over the next five years, in addition to seeing the birth of his son, he earned a master's degree, ministered as a youth pastor, traveled preaching and singing, worked as sales manager for a construction company, added credits toward a master of divinity degree, and again served as youth pastor. All of this was essential preparation for what lay ahead.

Being a senior pastor, with round-the-clock responsibilities including sermon preparation, decision making, prayer, meetings, planning, and counseling, is a daunting task to anyone. For years Ken wondered whether he could realistically shoulder such a role. In the spring of 1981 he felt ready to try. He talked to his superintendent and was encouraged to investigate a home-missions church in Bolingbrook, Illinois, a Chicago suburb. Several pastors had served there sacrificially for ten years and had established a beachhead—a congregation of twenty children and twenty adults—but they had been thwarted from achieving greater fruitfulness. After driving up for a look-see, Ken concluded this was more than he could handle. "I'd like something a little easier," he told his superintendent. "I've just been through a tough situation and don't need another."

God rarely leads us to easier responsibilities. The day after his thirtieth birthday Ken began as pastor in Bolingbrook. Leading a mission church is like pioneering in the wilderness, with all the necessities of life, usually taken for granted, lacking. "The people were discouraged," says Ken. "They wondered whether the church would make it. The finances were nil. My salary that first year was meager, and we had two kids as well as school debts and hospital bills hanging over us. The church met in a school that we could use only on Sunday mornings; any other meetings had to be scheduled elsewhere in town. In addition to my usual duties, I led worship—while playing the keyboard one-handed—taught Sunday school, and did the bookkeeping."

After a few crucial innovations, they began to see progress. "We started a Tuesday morning intercessory prayer group that met faithfully," remembers Ken. "In addition we hired a youth pastor, even though we didn't have a dime for him, which brought an influx of young people." Meanwhile the church's ministry began touching lives—healing marriages, leading people to faith in Christ, binding up broken hearts. After two years the sixty-member congregation bought three acres of property. Several years later they built a six thousand-square-foot facility. By 1990, nine years after Ken moved to Bolingbrook, the church numbered in the hundreds and had completed two building programs.

Ken knows where the credit belongs. At the same time, he knows how unexplainable it is that other equally faithful people don't enjoy visible blessings. "It just so happened that in His grace God blessed me." They can't all be explained, but clearly some rewards are here and now, others there and then.

God's Rewards Infinitely Outweigh the Hardships of Perseverance

One cold day Clarence Berry was going about his job as usual. The Yukon stove in the center of the fourteen-by-fifteen-foot log cabin was burning hot when a familiar face appeared, a man known as Lying George. By and by, as other grizzled prospectors mulled listlessly around, he raised his hand and shouted, "Boys, I've got some good news to tell you. There's a big strike up the river." He pulled from his pocket a used Winchester shotgun shell and poured its contents on the table: a pile of gold nuggets panned from Rabbit Creek days earlier.

The cabin emptied. Along with everyone else, Berry scampered for the area soon to be renamed "Bonanza." He arrived in time to pound stakes into a section flanking the creek and later recorded his claim at the land office.

Still, a few gold nuggets and a rush to stake claims was nothing new in this region; whether profitable amounts of gold would be uncovered remained unlikely. So he returned to work at Fortymile to keep food on the table, still a man on the brink of poverty.

One day he met a fellow named Stander who was in a pinch: He lacked money for provisions, yet claimed to have found gold on another tiny creek, the Eldorado. Berry offered help getting credit, and in return Stander traded half his claim on Eldorado for half of Berry's on Bonanza. Together they hurried out to Eldorado.

The only way to assess the value of their claim was to burrow down to bedrock, through fifteen feet of permafrost, which would take two months. Each day they cut and hauled wood for fires that would soften eight inches of the frozen gravel. Inch by inch, fire by fire, bucketful by bucketful of muck, they shoveled deeper, while other prospectors, made skeptical by past disappointments, jeered.

Weeks passed. One day, working by candlelight in the shaft, Berry finally hit bedrock. He scooped a panful of dirt and flushed water over it. What remained glistened. In that single pan was today's equivalent of $800 worth of gold. Deep in the permafrost, after years of futility, Berry had discovered the pay streak, a thick vein of gold that eventually netted him millions. Eldorado, a tiny stream in the forbidding frontier of Alaska, turned out to be the richest placer creek in the world.

For the persevering Christian, similar kingdom pay streaks await. As Paul said, "I consider that our present sufferings are not worth comparing with the glory that will be revealed to us" (Romans 8:18).

Although we don't hope for deep layers of permafrost to dig through, we can take multiplied satisfaction if that's our calling. Jesus told those harassed for His sake to "rejoice and be glad, because *great* is your reward in heaven . . ." (Matthew 5:12 italics added). It appears that the rewards of those who suffer for the kingdom will exceed what the more comfortable receive. So difficult perseverance of any kind—whether honoring a marriage covenant with a trying spouse or continuing to teach a Sunday school class of four rambunctious toddlers—is an action sure to earn comforting kingdom returns.

Rewards Can Be Forfeited by Quitting

With many projects, unless the process is finished, the work is wasted. A chef may spend hours making homemade bread—shopping for ingredients, mixing and kneading the dough, waiting for it to rise, then baking it in the oven—but if he takes it out too soon, the gooey center will earn it a place in the garbage. A gymnast can perform a perfect routine with sky-high difficulty and dynamic technique, yet if he stumbles during the dismount, it will cost him a trophy. An accountant may meticulously audit page after page of inventory records, accounts payable ledgers, and disbursement journals, but if he omits handing the board of directors a completed audit statement, he doesn't get paid. In such tasks, the finish is intrinsically, inseparably linked with the entire process.

Spiritually, persevering through the finale is no less necessary. The believer who apostatizes from the faith, even after years of churchgoing, forfeits salvation. If we bail out of an ordained trial, we lose the opportunity to fulfill divine objectives. If we scrap a scriptural promise, we abandon the blessings already accumulated.

Therefore, God cautions, "Watch out that you do not lose what you have worked for, but that you may be rewarded fully" (2 John 8). Note four cardinal principles in this verse about keeping or losing rewards:

1. *God wants us to be fully rewarded.* It's not as if we were earning a paycheck from a skinflint employer bent on reducing paychecks to the minimum. On the contrary, generosity motivates all of God's rewards, since while doing right we are only doing our duty. The Lord delights in opening His hand of blessing and takes no pleasure in anyone's forfeiting his rewards.

2. *It is possible to lose rewards.* Over recent years we have seen even Olympic gold medalists stripped of awards because of abuses like using steroids. Life teaches that full rewards always hinge on certain conditions, one being perseverance.

3. *Rewards may be partially, rather than wholly, lost.* Stumblers don't necessarily lose everything, for God is fair and generous. Nevertheless, faltering does at least diminish rewards.

4. *Others cannot steal our rewards; we only lose them ourselves.* This verse identifies the one who most threatens our treasures in heaven. It uses the word *lose*, which describes our own action. Our rewards are beyond pilfering by others, but not beyond losing by ourselves. We are the only enemy, and quitting is our ultimate weapon.

It is remarkable what a person can do for the sake of great rewards. No surprise, then, that throughout history believers have been able to endure hardships trifling or tragic, from loss of convenience to loss of life, for the sake of heavenly gold. Even the most grievous ordeals are infinitely outweighed by our Promised Land rewards. Although delayed, they so outshine the perks of this world that believers would persevere, if need be, for ten lifetimes.

And upon those who stand firm to the finish, God will bestow the consummate treasure: "Do not be afraid, Abram," God said in Genesis 15:1. "I am your shield, your very great reward." There is no richer compensation for the steadfast than God Himself, well-pleased with His child.

9
To See Prayer Answered

Perseverance is not all-powerful, though some sayings suggest otherwise. "Nothing in the world can take the place of persistence," said Calvin Coolidge. "Talent will not; nothing is more common than unsuccessful men of talent. Genius will not; unrewarded genius is almost a proverb. Education will not; the world is full of educated derelicts. Persistence and determination alone are omnipotent." As inspiring and as true as that is from a human perspective, in reality God alone is sovereign. Consequently, only by depending on Him can we guarantee perseverance is worthwhile.

Without God our tenacious efforts may be a total waste. People have spent lifetimes on pursuits that have fizzled. Yes, we can retell stories of Thomas Alva Edison and how he tried thousands of different filaments in his light bulb before finding the right one, but for every man like him there are scores who have persisted without success.

I don't believe ultimately in perseverance. I believe in God—and what He will do through our perseverance. One activity, therefore, becomes essential: prayer. God's bewildering promises apply not just to those who persevere, but those who pray and persevere. ". . . You do not have," says James 4:2, "because you do not ask God." So tangible changes in our circumstances depend on persisting—prayerfully.

Unfortunately the very people who try praying can become the most disillusioned. It happened to me. In my early years of pastoring in Chicago, we faced various desperate needs on a daily basis, and naturally I would pray. Sometimes the answers didn't come when or how I wanted. Of course, God faithfully met all our needs; but many of my expectations were frustrated. On those occasions my rock-ribbed confidence in prayer suffered a bruising.

The effect was small but devastating. Although I didn't whittle down my prayer time, usually at least an hour a day, I would omit asking for my deepest needs. When you need something critically, like healing or financial supply, but the answer doesn't come as desired, it triggers a huge emotional cave-in. Having had a few of those, I couldn't bear any more.

This lasted for six months or so. Meantime, like a virulent strep infection, some mistaken assumptions settled in while my resistance was low. I suspect these assumptions are as common as a cold, though far more debilitating. Here are five of them.

This Must Not Be God's Will

The wisest man of all time recognized well our problem. "A man's steps are directed by the Lord. How then can anyone understand his own way?" (Proverbs 20:24). Difficulties and seeming futility only amplify our confusion. In Chicago when I was knocking my head against the wall, on occasion I logically concluded, "I guess God doesn't want this church here, or me here. Somehow I must have missed His will." Others decide that God really doesn't want to provide, say, a job, a marriage partner, healing, financial provision, freedom from some bad habit, or material necessities. After all, sometimes the Lord does direct us through our circumstances.

Judging on that basis alone, however, is tricky and usually misleading. In 1 John 5:14, 15, verses that relate our three concerns—God's will, prayer, and time—we see why: "This is the confidence which we have before Him, that, if we ask anything according to His will, He hears us. And if we know that He hears us in whatever we ask, *we know that we have the requests which we have asked from Him*" (NAS, italics added).

A vital distinction: Is that last clause a statement of visible reality, or of faith? According to this Scripture, once we pray for something that is God's will, even though we don't hold it physically in our hands, somehow the answer to prayer is already ours—"we *have* the requests." But only by faith.

Consequently, we often confront a time delay in prayer. *Even when something is God's will*, the manifest answer is frequently detained. Nowhere does the Bible specify a standard lag, whether long or short, minutes or years, so a delay signals nothing, repeat *nothing*, about God's will. Therefore, if we unjustifiably assume, "This must not be God's will," because of a holdup, we most likely are losing what is already, somehow, mysteriously, ours.

Better insight into this mystery will prevent false assumptions. How can the Bible claim, without getting into word games or doublespeak, that we already—truly—have something that we cannot yet see? (For a related Scripture read Mark 11:23, 24.) I suggest the key is to know not just when, but where, we possess answers to prayer.

God's throne is in heaven. There He listens to our prayers and with unsearchable wisdom decides how to answer. Once the Almighty says yes, there in heaven, it is somehow spiritually a solid reality, a fait accompli. God's sovereignty and purposes are so great that His "mere" intention to act can be relied upon and viewed as an actual fact, as surely as the ground we walk on. "Surely, as I have planned, so it will be," God says in Isaiah 14:24, "and as I have purposed, so it will stand." Things decreed by God in heaven are very, very real.

Here on earth the answer may continue unseen. But those who walk by faith, not sight, know that heaven's realities will one day supersede earth's. Perhaps this is partly the sense of our Lord's Prayer, "May Your will be done on earth as it is in heaven." In other words, "May Your purposes be fulfilled here on the earth." In a sense, God wants us to pray heaven down to earth. I call it the two dimensions of prayer.

However long that takes, God authorizes us to count heaven's reality as our immediate possession. We can speak with the confidence of a boy approaching Christmas, who for months has been asking his parents for a bike and tells all his pals, "I'm getting a bike for Christmas." Though unable to see or ride it yet, he knows it's in the attic. Having to wait for December 25 doesn't faze his conviction in the least.

Doubt over God's will was my first mistaken assumption. My second was:

If It Were Going to Happen, It Would Have Happened by Now

At times I thought, *I've been praying the same prayer for three years, and little has changed. This is a waste of breath.* When this error befalls us, we assume that God simply cannot expect us to wait beyond some reasonable time frame. We enact a spiritual statute of limitations, presuming our prayers must be answered within, say, three months, or they lose their jurisdiction. Time becomes an opponent, more the arbiter of reality than God's Word. With each passing day our prayers and faith weaken, doomed to the life span of a mayfly.

Acute crises, such as a child dying of heart disease, can certainly intensify this feeling.

The hospital conference room was stark: white table, green chalkboard, eight chairs. Vince and Teri sat down with the heart surgeon after the second operation for a briefing on Rebekah's future. The doctor, a tall, balding man in his fifties, moved to the chalkboard and drew a picture of her heart. "We'll have to wait several months," he said, "and see what happens to the pulmonary veins. If they begin to close again, there's no sense in attempting the final surgery."

Obviously her prognosis was still riddled with ominous question marks. "The second surgery was just a Band-Aid," says Vince. "They didn't expect that emergency with her veins." In effect they were merely treading water.

Over the following weeks, Teri often wrestled with the feeling that time was running out. She would walk into the nursery, see her baby sleeping, and think of the painful procedures ahead, the risks, the tears. Frequently she knelt by the crib and after crying for a while would pray, "Lord, nothing is too hard for You. Don't let her go through any more of this. The recovery is so awful. Please heal Rebekah without surgery. Touch her heart and let everyone see Your power."

Months passed, and finally the doctors scheduled Rebekah's fourth cardio-cath exam. During the procedure the mood in the waiting room was upbeat. After the third hour passed without report (it was supposed to last only two hours), tension mounted. "We knew that either the miracle was happening and they were all amazed," says Vince, "or something terrible was happening."

At long last the cardiologist came out to report: For three hours they had been trying to insert the testing instrument into her veins, first in one leg, then the other, then her arm, without success. "We've called in another cardiologist," he concluded, "and tomorrow we'll try again."

Teri's first reaction: *Uh, uh,* she thought. *No way: I'm not going to put up with this. You're not chopping up my baby.* They asked, "How sure are you that this doctor's going to be able to get in?"

"We're not sure," replied the surgeon. "But we cannot schedule surgery without seeing these veins." Vince and Teri had no options, and tomorrow arrived quickly.

This time the mood was different. After two hours, Vince, restless and impatient, walked out and asked the nurse whether she had heard anything. "Yes," she said, "the doctor was just here looking for you." At the other end of a long hall they saw him, a short, gray-haired man wearing a gray lab coat, walking toward them.

With few words and no emotion, he informed them that he had succeeded. "The blood flow looks good," he said. "The veins are open. You can do the surgery." Almost grimly, he walked away. He knew, all too well, that what lay ahead was nothing to get excited about.

* * *

The assumption "If it was going to happen, it would have happened by now" sometimes results from losing sight of how God has designed prayer to work. He does give us extraordinary latitude. His open-ended promises include "Ask and it will be given to you," "According to your faith will it be done to you," and "Nothing is impossible with God." Faced with such overwhelming possibilities, in effect handed a nearly blank check, we can grow headstrong and expect too much, getting angry because God retains the right to pen in the date. Although through our prayers the sovereign God invites finite humans to join in determining what will happen on earth to an unbelievable extent, He reserves the exclusive right to determine when.

The Bible never sets a statute of limitation on prayer. On the contrary, the passing of time draws it closer to perfection. Look at the story of Elijah praying on Mount Carmel. Because of a long drought in Israel, the prophet had put his face between his knees to ask God for rain. Eventually he lifted his head and told his servant, "Go and look toward the sea." The man walked, looked, saw neither clouds nor rain, came back, and reported Elijah's failure in prayer.

Elijah said, "Go back." The man walked, looked, saw neither clouds nor rain, came back, and reported accordingly.

Again Elijah told him, "Go back." Again, nothing. For the fourth time he ordered, "Go back." Then the fifth time . . . and the sixth. Finally on the seventh trip, the servant spotted a little puff in the sky no bigger than a man's hand. Quickly the cloud expanded, darkened, and unleashed a thunderstorm that restored life to the land.

This drama numerically portrays the perfect perseverance required for answered prayer. Elijah prayed and persisted seven times—the number that symbolizes perfection in the Bible—in looking and waiting for rain. The span of our perseverance will vary, from ten minutes to ten years, from one prayer to one thousand, but the principle remains the same: We must keep looking, waiting, and praying until perfection is reached.

We hate to wait. Everything in modern culture is geared toward minimizing delay for consumers, to where we expect the same in spiritual things. But haste results in missing what God wants to give. Isaiah 64:4 says He "acts on behalf of those who wait for him."

My third mistaken assumption was:

If It's God's Will, He'll Do It Whether I Pray or Not

It was easy for me to fall prey to fatalism. Sometimes even though I didn't pray, God would bless my efforts; at other times I sought the Lord fervently, only to come up dry. On a few occasions I caught myself thinking, *God has this thing planned out. My prayers don't affect it very much.* Such deterministic thinking suffocates prayer.

Some big questions, then: Do our prayers really affect God's plans? Also, do persistent prayers, offered day after day, make any difference? In other words, granted, God may want to hear that first request, but if that gets no response, aren't we just bucking the system?

Jesus told a little story that addresses these questions (and I have used my imagination to fill in a few of the blanks; *see* Luke 11:5–8). A man was in a bind: A friend had popped in for a surprise visit late at night, catching him with the cupboards bare. (Even McDonald's had closed!) So he decided to risk something. Though near midnight, he walked over to his neighbor's house, having been on good terms for several years, and knocked on the door. After a long pause the man inside asked, "Who is it?"

He answered, "Friend, lend me three loaves of bread, because a friend of mine on a journey has come to me, and I have nothing to set before him."

The neighbor was unimpressed. In fact, he was cranky. "Don't bother me," he said.

Well, that's that. No one wants to antagonize the person next door. But this man was desperate. He knocked again, loudly. "Go away," the neighbor yelled.

"Please, I need some bread. Can't you just give me three loaves?"

"It's midnight," shouted the neighbor. "You are the most inconsiderate person I've ever met. Get lost!"

Intimidated, the man paused, turned and walked a few steps, paused again, then went back to the door, and knocked softly. "I'm sorry to bother you," he said meekly, "and I'll do any favor you ask, but, please, help out. My guest is famished."

Inside, quiet. Then suddenly the door flew open. Three loaves of bread hit him in the stomach and dropped to the ground, and just as quickly the door slammed shut.

Getting to the point, Jesus said, "Though he [the neighbor] will not get up and give him anything because he is his friend, yet because of his *persistence* he will get up and give him as much as he needs" (Luke 11:8 NAS, italics added). Note the three influential factors that surprisingly proved unpersuasive on this occasion: a relationship (his friend), a need (no food), and a request ("lend me three loaves"). Ultimately the clincher was *persistence*.

In the very next verse, Jesus applied this bread story to our prayers: "So I say to you, Ask and keep on asking, and it shall be given you; seek and keep on seeking, and you shall find; knock and keep on knocking, and the door shall be opened to you" (Luke 11:9 quoted from the Amplified Bible, which highlights the special ongoing verb tense of the original Greek). Clearly, persistence is a factor in prayer. Yes, we enjoy a loving relationship with God; yes, we may face pressing needs for which He promises to provide; yes, we may have already asked Him once—but we are still told to persist. I cannot say, "If it's God's will, He'll do it whether I pray or not." If persistence compels a response from even cranky neighbors, how much more from our heavenly, compassionate, untiring Father.

In addition to the error of fatalism, my fourth mistaken assumption was:

God Doesn't Care

Despite knowing in my head that God loved me, in my heart the feeling lurked unspoken, perhaps unthought, that God didn't care about my problems. This was a thoroughly logical conclusion, from a human point of view. If, for example, I shared my need with another person and was apparently ignored, I would conclude they didn't care. Good theology or not, sometimes it's hard not to think that way about the Lord.

We may even view God as acting like the cranky neighbor in the parable (by the way, Jesus didn't tell this story to portray how God truly acts and feels, rather, to show that persistence brings results even with the uncaring). To ensure that no one misunderstood God's love, Jesus plainly revealed God's true sentiments, in the following verses, Luke 11:11–13:

> Which of you fathers, if your son asks for a fish, will give him a snake instead? Or if he asks for an egg, will give him a scorpion? If you then, though you

are evil, know how to give good gifts to your children, how much more will your Father in heaven give the Holy Spirit to those who ask him!

The parallel passage in Matthew 7:11 says, "How much more will your Father in heaven give good gifts to those who ask him!"

God tenderly succors us like a father his little children. Yet even this warm analogy ices over the hot truth, for hard-hearted fathers abound in the world, and even the good ones, says Jesus, are tainted by evil—by selfishness and unfaithfulness. God, on the other hand, is infinitely good, infinitely gracious, infinitely loving, infinitely generous. "As a father has compassion on his children," says Psalm 103:13, "so the Lord has compassion on those who fear him." My desire to buy my sons everything on their Christmas list is feeble compared to God's determination to shower His children with blessings.

In Luke 11:5–13, Jesus has juxtaposed two teachings that mix like oil and water: (a) We must persist in prayer, since persistence persuades even the disinclined, and (b) God loves His children more than the best of fathers and would give all beneficial gifts. The coupling of these contradictions teaches two lessons:

1. *When God requires perseverance from us, it doesn't mean He lacks concern.* It may feel that way. It would seem so if another person acted similarly, but it's not true of God because

2. *His very love is what motivates His delay.* In some instances if God granted our request immediately, it would profit us

less, even harm us. He waits in wisdom. For example, sometimes an earthly father delays answering his son's request because he wants him to gain priceless character through an experience, sometimes to prevent him from getting spoiled or misdirected, sometimes to coordinate with other people, financial factors, or situations.

A loving father's ultimate concern is to strengthen family ties. He says, "Wait," to the child who wants to do things himself without waiting for Dad's free time. Or, neglecting our side of the relationship, we may approach God only for emergencies. By encouraging prayer-perseverance, God fosters communication and bonds with His children. Love and concern for our well-being motivates all paternal patience.

My final mistaken assumption was:

I've Repeated This Prayer Enough Times

Here it was not just how long I had prayed but how often. How many times did the Lord want to hear this? When have we prayed enough? Should we ever stop requesting and simply rest on faith?

Apparently not. "Then Jesus told his disciples a parable," says Luke 18:1, "to show them that they should *always pray and not give up*" (emphasis mine).

Some have suggested that repetition in prayer signifies weak faith. On the contrary, in another story we read that Jesus considered it a sign of great faith! During His journey through the Gentile region of Tyre and Sidon, a Canaanite woman pleaded with Him to minister to her daughter. Jesus remained mum. A second time she asked, kneeling and begging, "Lord, help me!"

Again Jesus refused. Finally, a third time she pressed her

plea. "Then Jesus answered, 'Woman, *you have great faith! Your request is granted.'* And her daughter was healed from that very hour" (Matthew 15:28 emphasis mine). Far from symptomizing anemia, perseverance in prayer actually reflects vigor, desire, "great faith."

The real infirmity is to lose confidence in prayer, as I did for several months. But over time God cured my misconceptions. One by one He answered my smaller requests, emboldening me to stretch my faith. As many larger petitions were answered, and as my thoughts were restored by the daily reading of God's Word, my confidence in prayer returned and then surpassed previous levels. Today my philosophy of ministry stands on one pillar: prayer. More than that, perseverance in prayer. Just as Elijah kept sending his servant to look for a cloud on the horizon, I'm going to keep praying, waiting, working, and waiting.

*   *   *

Holding white-knuckled to the rail, Vince, Teri, and Rebekah swung into the final leg of the roller coaster. Over the next eight weeks, they continued to pray for healing and encouraged everyone around them to trust the Lord for a miracle. Yet some warned against such prayers; if anything went wrong, they worried, Vince and Teri were setting themselves up for a breakdown. Nevertheless, hoping God would spare Rebekah from the pain, Daddy and Mommy persisted.

The days ticked off. Finally, even after many prayers, it was the night before surgery. Calm panic began setting in. Before putting Rebekah to bed, Teri anxiously danced with her in their hospital room, quoting Scripture and singing God's praises. *God, I'm getting nervous,* Teri prayed, *I'm getting scared. I know she's going to be healed, but it looks like she'll have to go through this surgery.* "I just wanted to cry," remembers Teri. Then her thoughts veered with a sudden inspiration. "Spontaneously I started to sing a song about angels. I was just making it up I guess." She opened her Bible to Psalm 91 and read it to Rebekah. "He will command his angels concerning you to guard you in all your ways" (v. 11). The peace of God blanketed Teri's heart, and she tucked her baby in bed.

Shortly, she herself lay down. Then without warning it happened. Moments after closing her eyes and before falling asleep Teri suddenly saw a clear picture: "I saw angels all around the operating room, over the doctors' shoulders, in back of them, all lined up against the wall. There were tons of them. And then there was this giant angel, with a big sword, standing right above her head, and he was holding the sword up." Fleeting moments later, it ended. Greatly encouraged, Teri fell quickly to sleep.

It was a quiet summer morning with sunshine and a few clouds; just after dawn Vince drove north on Lake Shore Drive through Chicago. The hospital, shining in the morning glow, was already a beehive of doctors, nurses, patients, and parents. He rode the elevator to the third floor. A short time later the nurses wheeled eleven-month-old Rebekah—still weighing only ten pounds but with blondish brown, curly hair now three inches long—down to the second-floor operating room with her parents at her side. They had taped a new Scripture to her bed: "I will not die but live, and will proclaim what the Lord has done" (Psalm 118:17).

The operation was projected to last eight hours. After incision and the opening of Rebekah's chest cavity, the surgical team cooled her body down to twenty-one degrees. Then they transferred her vital functions to the heart-lung machine, which enabled them to stop her heart and begin repairs: Like tailors, the doctors meticulously sewed a high-tech fabric into the two defect holes, then separated her double right outlets, and gently expanded her pulmonary veins. All Rebekah's vital signs were remaining uncommonly stable. The operating room was crowded, uncommonly crowded.

Hours later they warmed Rebekah's body back to normal temperature. At the moment of truth—restarting her heartbeat—they held their breath . . . pushed the button sending an electrical charge into her white, still body and watched. With a flourish, her heart raced back to life. Slowly, deliberately, they closed her chest and stitched her baby-soft skin together. For the first time, Rebekah's blood was flowing normally. Everyone in OR was pleased.

Four days afterward, Teri tenderly cradled the answer to her prayers. *Lord, You have done this,* her heart overflowed. *You have brought Rebekah through. You have done miraculous things. Thank You, Jesus.* Standing at her side in wonder, Vince's emotion could only be expressed in soft touches and simple repetition, "Hello, Rebekah . . . Hi, Rebekah . . . How's Rebekah . . . Hello, Rebekah. . . ."

"Oh, Rebekah," Teri gushed, "you're going to be healthy, you're going to be strong, you'll go to school, you'll climb trees, because our God is mighty, so mighty!"

The long, jolting ride was over. The big celebration was one month away.

10
To Pass the Test

During final-exams week students suffer vicious migraines and bloodshot eyes. At the state drivers' testing center, many line up in a cold sweat. Job aptitude tests and college entrance exams rob others of sleep. Few people, in short, enjoy a test, and with good reason.

Tests mean acceptance or rejection, pass or fail, promotion or stagnation. At stake is nothing less than our future, even our self-worth. Tests, therefore, demand peak performance and tedious preparation. Tests, in every sense of the word, are a crisis.

It's no surprise, then, that some choke on Scriptures like Proverbs 17:3, "The crucible for silver and the furnace for gold, but the Lord tests the heart." What? God tests us? Aren't we accepted in Christ? Don't we stand under grace, not law? Must we perform for our loving heavenly Father? Furthermore, since God knows everything, why test?

The fact is, even fathers test their sons, thankfully with a different attitude than the drivers' license examiner. In this chapter we will answer three questions: First, why does God test us? Second, how? Third, how can I be sure to pass each test?

Why Does God Test Us?

Moses explained the Lord's purpose for testing His beloved people in Deuteronomy 8:16, "He gave you manna to eat in the desert, something your fathers had never known, to humble and to test you *SO THAT IN THE END IT MIGHT GO WELL WITH YOU*" (italics and caps added). As always our loving, wise Father is pursuing our highest good, our greatest blessing.

God loves us enough to allow beneficial pain. Sometimes parents overprotect a child more from selfishness than love, in reality sparing themselves the pain of seeing their child hurt. But a concerned and farsighted parent willingly suffers with the child, for example when she receives a tetanus shot, for the sake of her protection. God knows tests hurt, but in love He allows them for our good, at His own personal cost. "In all their distress he too was distressed . . ." (Isaiah 63:9).

But how are tests good? I see four solid benefits.

1. *A Test Can Prevent Disaster*

Test pilots base their careers, and safety, on this principle. Before they climb into the cockpit of a prototype for its first flight, the plane has already undergone thousands of ground tests. Wind tunnels reveal aerodynamic characteristics. Ovens test heat resiliency. Acoustic chambers examine the effects of high-frequency engine noise on structures. Rapid cycle vibrators investigate wing-panel flutter. Hydraulic jacks push, bend, and twist the airplane. Engines undergo propulsion research. Finally the test pilot begins his flight program, first with ground-taxi tests, then brief flights at the low end of the performance spectrum, then longer flights that deliberately push the aircraft to the limits. Through such shakedown missions, engineers seek to discover and correct weaknesses, thereby preventing a crash.

When it comes to kinks in aircraft, ignorance is never bliss. God knows the same is true of our character. Just as a plane's aerodynamics, sound or flawed, determine whether it will soar or stall, so character is destiny. People crash daily because of major personal faults, hurting not only themselves but also innocent bystanders. Unfortunately until a test or crash landing alerts us, we are unaware of most weaknesses.

It was Sunday afternoon. A pastor and his wife came home from church feeling less than blessed. Because of the church's building program, as well as adapting themselves to a new baby, they were physically exhausted and emotionally spent, a bad time to talk about anything.

But, of course, they did. "I can't be a pastor's wife," Ann said. "You're never home. The church takes all your time. I have to care for three kids alone. On top of that, people in church criticize me, 'Why aren't you leading songs, why aren't you singing in the choir, why aren't you teaching Sunday school, why aren't you running the ladies' Bible study?' And then from you I hear, 'Why can't you be like Pastor Neal's wife?' "

Peter was in no mood for pastoral evaluation. "All these years I'm working for this ministry," he shouted back, "and all these years I'm building credibility, and now you're going to leave me. You'll look all right, you'll be with the kids, and I'll be alone and out of the ministry. Is that what you want?"

By this time Ann had pulled up almost eyeball-to-eyeball with him. "I don't know what I want," she said. "But that's how I feel!"

In the white heat of the moment, he yelled, "Just get away from me," and, in a terrifying reflex, butted her face with his forehead. Never in fourteen years of marriage had he struck her. There was a popping sound, and her nose began to gush blood. She rushed to the bathroom sobbing.

He panicked. He was sure her nose was broken, that she would have two black eyes as a result. "Oh dear God, I'm sorry," he blurted. "Lord, please forgive me. Please heal her. Don't let it be broken."

He hurried repentantly into the bathroom. "Ann, I'm sorry," he pleaded. "I didn't mean to do it. Please forgive me."

Before long her nose stopped bleeding, and they realized it wouldn't be serious. They went into the living room and for the rest of the afternoon talked and prayed. "This was dangerous," Peter said. "I really could have hurt you. I could have broken your nose. Look what we're doing. I might build beautiful buildings and have a church of a thousand, but what good is that if you and I are not together. If we're just fighting like this, and you keep feeling like quitting the ministry, and I keep making you stay, it's just not worth it."

Peter looks back on that crisis now and sees it as a lifesaver. "That day was a turning point. We determined from that time on that we were going to build our family. I determined that I would be a better father, spend more time with her and the kids, and not put so many pressures on her. I recommitted myself, and she recommitted herself."

Albeit traumatic, that trial has had far-reaching benefits. "Since then God has helped us," Peter continues. "We've had a cohesiveness and bonding. We've joined each other's team. There's more peace, more of an understanding. Our marriage is better now than it's ever been." Tests—even those of our own making—can indeed prevent future disasters. But they do more than that.

2. A Test Prepares Us for Future Achievement

Budding athletes, for instance, flourish under the test of competition. After training for two years, my oldest son, Aaron, competed in his first official gymnastics meet, and I saw two striking effects on him. First, he told me afterward, "I thought I would score eights right away, that it would be easy. Then I saw how hard it was to score even sevens and realized how much I need to work on." Second, when he hit his routines under pressure, his confidence increased. Now he practices with a new assurance, more aware of his abilities and goals.

By passing tests, Christians also flourish visibly, expansively. We learn that God indeed answers prayer, that His promises stand truly reliable, that He is absolutely faithful. Until we place everything on the line and see God come through, it's only theory, and static theory at that. But proven faith increases, preparing us for future service on a larger scale.

God doesn't start anyone on a giant scale, not even David. Although we might think that Goliath posed a mammoth first test for him, listen to David explain why he, though never a warrior, would confidently face the Philistine:

Your servant has been keeping his father's sheep. When a lion or a bear came and carried off a sheep from the flock, I went after it, struck it and rescued the sheep from its mouth. When it turned on me, I seized it by its hair, struck it and killed it. Your servant has killed both the lion and the bear; this uncircumcised Philistine will be like one of them. . . . The Lord who delivered me from the paw of the lion and the paw of the bear will deliver me from the hand of this Philistine.

1 Samuel 17:34–37

David's beastly wrestling matches were hardly random occurrences; rather they were tests sent by God to prepare him for Goliath. For believers, every test is prep school.

3. A Test Proves Us Worthy of a Crown

Worth must be proven. Just as gold is assayed, for example, by rubbing it on a black siliceous touchstone and then comparing the rubbing of a known pure gold, so anything of value is proved bona fide by a test, whether a lawyer tested by the bar exam, a new car tested by quality-control engineers, or a property deed tested by a title search. For forty days in the desert, even Jesus faced the acid test.

In a spiritual test, ironically, we feel like rejects, as if God doesn't value us. Precisely the opposite is true, as the previous example of Jesus shows. "Blessed is the man who perseveres under trial," says James 1:12, "because when he has stood the test, he will receive the crown of life that God has promised to those who love him." A test signifies that God intends to crown us.

4. Testing Refines Us of Impurities

Testing does more than examine; it purifies. The more valuable the article, the less we tolerate impurities. In dirt we expect to have worms, fungus, ants, maggots, and bacteria. In our gold and silver, on the other hand, we demand purity. The metalsmiths of biblical times refined gold and silver in furnaces drafted by air bellows. After it melted, the dross would float to the top and be skimmed or blown away. Refined gold naturally sold at premium prices.

This process illustrates God's craftsmanship of the soul. "See, I have *refined* you, though not as silver; I have *tested* you in the furnace of affliction" (Isaiah 48:10 italics added). A test is a well-drafted spiritual blast furnace, with the purpose being progress not pain, purity not punishment. God knows that dross harms, cheapens, and corrupts us, while holiness brings life, health, favor, peace, and happiness.

Why does God test us? Because in love He seeks our true prosperity. Thus we can enter a test positively, alert for the good in store.

Just as students benefit by knowing whether an exam will be essay or multiple choice, so do we by knowing types of spiritual tests.

How Does God Test Us?

Scripture reveals four broad categories.

The Test of Time

Some call time the acid test. Paint companies employ this one in their ads. Using a split screen and time-lapse photography, they compare their product with brand X. After one year, both houses glisten. After two, brand X begins to crack and bubble. After three years, it is flaking, while the good stuff shines on.

Brand-X responses to the test of time were King Saul's bitter specialty. Newly anointed by Samuel as king of Israel, he quickly encountered his first test: An enemy had besieged an Israeli city east of the Jordan River. Saul sternly challenged his people—threatening to butcher the oxen of draft dodgers—and soon everyone rallied, successfully repelling the foe. A+ for Saul.

Definition of a general: a man who "finds a way or makes a way." Recall, as outlined in chapter 2, that the Philistines later swept into the land. When his outgunned army began drifting away in the moonlight, General Saul desperately sought something to stem the tide, and overstepped his authority: He offered a sacrifice in direct disobedience to God's command. Samuel read him the riot act.

But God gave him another chance, dispatching him on another mission. Nevertheless, oblivious to God's orders, Saul again caved in to pressure.

To use a baseball analogy, Saul had been a spring phenom, batting .450, but by the all-star break, he was warming the bench. The moral: While starting well is important, finishing well is red-letter imperative. The person who would pass the test of time guards against midseason slumps and September boredom, determined to post a winning record on the last day of the season.

The Test of Stress

This trial, usually densely compressed, is the opposite of the thin, enervating test of time. Stress testing, such as overloading an old bridge to discover cracks in the structural steel, reveals what normalcy hides. In like manner, under the stress of problems, hardships, trials, and temptations, our heart of hearts bleeds forth.

Abraham, who by waiting twenty-five years for Isaac's birth had already aced the test of time, also faced a killer of a stress test. Genesis 22:1 says, "Some time later God tested Abraham. . . ." He told him to sacrifice Isaac on Mount Moriah. As incomprehensible as this is to us now—and was to him then—Abraham obeyed, saddling his donkey, taking his son, climbing the mountain, even grasping, with trembling fingers, the knife. But then the Lord interrupted him, directing that a ram be sacrificed in the boy's place.

Interesting that the angel of the Lord said, ". . . *Now I know* that you fear God . . ." (v. 12). Tests reveal much about us. Interesting, too, that Abraham didn't have to kill his son. When God tests, He also provides, as Abraham testified by naming that mountain, "The Lord will provide" (*Yahweh Jireh*). Knowing that if left to our own power we would fail, the Lord never leaves us in the lurch but provides however necessary. Unlike a pilot getting his license, we never fly solo. In fact, the ultimate question in every test is whether we will rely on God, not ourselves. A related verse promises, ". . . God is faithful; he will not let you be tempted beyond what you can bear. But when you are tempted, he will also provide a way out so that you can stand up under it" (1 Corinthians 10:13).

Stress tests are an exercise in divine love. Far from seeking merely to point out the cracks in us, the Lord supremely wants to weld them with His power. Hence, for a passing grade, we need only to rely on the Lord completely and obey without reserve.

The Test of Lack

In baseball, for example, even first-round draft choices are tested by the minor leagues. There they play in secondhand uniforms on fields with poor lighting and bumpy turf. The locker rooms resemble the YMCA rather than the country club. Teams travel by bus, not plane, and compete before hundreds, not thousands. Generally their paychecks are also minor league. Unless a player either loves baseball or will likely advance to the majors, he shortly hangs up his cleats. Thus, shortages test one's values and priorities.

All Christians play in the minor leagues at various times. Although God promises to meet all our needs, He does allow hand-to-mouth periods. One of the most significant miracles in the Old Testament, daily manna on the surface of the desert, was ordained as just such a test, as Moses later explained:

> Remember how the Lord your God led you all the way in the desert these forty years, to humble you and *to test you* in order to know what was in your heart, whether or not you would keep his commands. He humbled you, *causing you to hunger and then feeding you with manna.* . . .
> Deuteronomy 8:2, 3 (italics added)

Shortages tested whether a person loved God or only the blessings of God. God always fed them, but one day at a time.

As a result most flunked the test, complaining and planning how to return to Egypt instead of humbling themselves and praying for food. Similarly in our lives, the Lord may allow times of need to surface our true values, priorities, and allegiances.

In His infinite goodness, God always intends prosperity and well-being in the end. To achieve that, He must occasionally turn over a rock in our heart, bring to light the vermin underneath, then cleanse away these pernicious values and priorities (like idols, they distance us from God and lead to death). When tested by shortages, then, we pass first by avoiding disillusionment and second by heeding the words of the old gospel hymn, "Trust and Obey."

The Test of Prosperity

Prosperity may be the most challenging test of all. Ball players face it when rewarded for stardom with lucrative multi-year contracts. On the surface this appears good for the players, but experience has often shown otherwise. Distractions—contracts, agents, commercials, investments, new businesses, new homes, new cars—divert their concentration from the game. Motivation slackens and discipline suffers. Few humans can stand success.

Three thousand years ago Moses understood this sad phenomenon. Having explained why Israel had suffered shortages, Moses warned of the equally stiff test ahead,

> The Lord your God is bringing you into a good
> land. . . . Be careful that you do not forget the Lord
> your God. . . . otherwise, when you eat and are
> satisfied, when you build fine houses and settle

down . . . then your heart will become proud and you will forget the Lord your God. . . .

Deuteronomy 8:7, 11–14

This test occurs because of God's irrepressible goodness, His sun shining on both the just and unjust.

Christians in prosperous lands run this cushy gauntlet daily. Only by constant vigilance against complacency, pride, self-sufficiency, worldly values, and temporal priorities can we overcome. If we cooperate, God will always help us, though, with perhaps the most difficult miracle of all: pulling a camel through the eye of a needle.

These four tests—of time, stress, lack, and prosperity—while graciously intended for our highest good, are nonetheless rigorous. How can we be sure to pass every one?

How Can I Pass the Test?

The Lord marches us triumphantly through tests in many ways, among the most important, by giving wisdom and hope. James 1:12 contains both:

Blessed is the man
who perseveres under trial,
because when he has stood the test,
he will receive the crown of life
that God has promised to those who love him.

Seven principles herein equip us to pass with honors every spiritual exam:

1. *Trials are tests.* Knowing what's happening is half the battle. Upon recognition we approach with vigilance, preparation, prayer, energy, and understanding, just as we would undertake an open-book exam differently from homework.

2. *The challenge of every test is to stand.* Here we see what constitutes failure or success. Trials tend to knock us off our feet, to unbalance our faith, commitment, understanding, direction. Therefore, as a boxer braces himself lest any blow drive him to the canvas, so we arm ourselves with a single resolve: No matter what, we will stand steadfast and immovable.

3. *Perseverance is the key to passing every test.* Note well the one qualification we cannot do without: "the man who *perseveres* under trial." To fail any test, quit early. That's the nature of testing. You can't answer only half the questions and expect to pass. You can't play only half the game and expect to win. You can't complete only half the application and expect a job. Trials and tests vary by the hundreds, but one constant is always required: finishing.

4. *Blessing follows testing.* According to this Scripture, testing precedes three pleasant things. First, it ushers in blessing and happiness. "Blessed is the man. . . ." Just as a higher paying career follows graduation, so kingdom blessings follow testing. God promises that happiness will eventually replace the sorrow.

5. *Crowning follows testing.* In addition we can expect honor. In athletics the awards ceremony follows competition. In the military the soldiers receive medals after the battle.

6. *Abundant life follows testing.* Tests can fool us. They feel like death, replete with pain, uncertainty, and loss. But in the end they bring something quite different: "He will receive the crown of life. . . ." Tests precede a quality of life that only God the Creator and Lifesource can give, abundant and full.

7. *A test is a bridge.* The Lord ordains distinct stages in our lives. At the transition points from one stage to the next, God builds bridges: tests. They are engineered not as barriers, but as passageways.

Jesus, for instance, immediately before beginning His four years of ministry, was led by God into the desert for forty days of testing. David, between the stages of successful military ventures and later kingly authority, wandered as a fugitive for years. These are flesh-and-blood examples of a principle, clearly stated in 1 Timothy 3:10, that guides how the Lord promotes His people: "They must first be tested. . . ." This verse concerned the selection of church deacons, but it reflects God's fundamental approach to moving anyone from one stage to the next. Tests, therefore, are bridges, doorways, transitions between stages of growth, ministry, and fruitfulness, which inspire bright hope.

Although tests feel like the end of everything, they are actually the beginning, a window of opportunity. They do conclude one stage of our lives, only to introduce the next.

Progress, therefore, depends on perseverance. Only by completing tests successfully can we reach the next stage.

Tests are indeed crises, but good ones. Early in 1989 my

family faced a critical moment. In the middle of the night, I drove my wife, who was in pain, to the hospital. The longer she was there, the worse the pain grew. Finally the doctor had no other choice. They wheeled her down the hall to a well-lit, sterilized room, where she gave birth to our fourth son, Brian David.

Like labor, tests can bring serious pain, but in the end, great joy and new life.

11
To Prove Faithful

Persevering can get boring, very boring. By definition it involves repetition and tedious continuity. Consequently, even the most important task may sooner or later feel mundane, worse yet, meaningless.

We on the other hand yearn to be unique. We want to set the untouchable record, cook the most popular pie, land the prestigious job, be the indispensable person. In our wildest dreams we envision biographers begging for the rights to our story. Thinking a bit more realistically, we at least would like to be mentioned occasionally in the local newspaper or envied at the coffee klatch. We want to be someone special, do something special, say something special.

This teeming world, however, grants that rarely, if at all, and to a select few. That is, if we judge by its standards. In the world you are somebody if you appear on TV, radio, or in print. You breathe rarefied air if you earn mounds of money, win a competition, or ascend to the pinnacle of power.

Thankfully the shallow standards of this world are overshadowed by a higher measure. The Bible lauds another kind of person, so unique as to be near extinct. ". . . A faithful man," asks Proverbs 20:6, "who can find?" Faithful people are more distinguished than Olympic champions. Not that faithfulness is impossible or achievable only by gifted servants or leaders. On the contrary, in Christ anyone can do it and is expected to. Faithfulness is rare because of what it requires.

Like Velcro, a faithful person sticks and clings to the valuable things in life, while an unfaithful person, like Teflon, lets them conveniently slide off. We are called to imitate God, who adheres to His words, covenants, promises, people, and righteousness.

Obviously, we can't cling like Velcro without persevering. Faithfulness requires perseverance in three facets of life: relationships, promises, and responsibilities. If we desert an ordained relationship, break a promise, or neglect our responsibilities, we become unfaithful.

Not only are faithful people special, they are also in great demand. Faithful people top our most-wanted lists for spouse, employee, neighbor, business associate, friend, church worker. We all want those around us to be loyal, word-keeping, and dependable, and upon finding them we prize them, as Proverbs 3:3, 4 says, "Let love and *faithfulness* never leave you. . . . *Then you will win favor and a good name* in the sight of God and man" (emphasis mine).

Let's examine in more instructive detail the three ways faithful people persevere.

Relationships

With poor balance due to his handicap, Ken Dignan has taken a lot of falls in his life. This one was somewhat out of the ordinary. Late one evening while cleaning up in the bathroom, he misstepped on the mat, hit the tile floor, and almost knocked himself out cold.

Joni rushed in to help. She struggled unsuccessfully to hoist him to his feet, while Ken suffered increasing pain in the back of his head as well as dizziness. Finally he crawled to his bed, and with Joni's help, he rolled onto it. Despite a good-sized bump, Ken soon fell asleep: a day in the life of the Dignans.

When he awoke, however, the room was a merry-go-round. He told Joni to call the paramedics.

"I was hesitant," she recalls. "I felt I could take him to the hospital or doctor myself if necessary. In addition, since this has happened many times before, I didn't think it was any different from the other times, or that the doctors could do anything for dizziness."

Nevertheless, she called. In minutes the ambulance arrived, lights flashing, and parked in front of the house. "I'm a very private person," says Joni. "Calling attention to ourselves embarrasses me. Ken normally does so well that you almost forget he's handicapped, and when something like this happens, I sometimes struggle with it. If possible, I just want to act like everything is normal."

The paramedics talked to Ken for a while, as neighbors gathered outside, then wheeled him on a stretcher into the ambulance, where they monitored him for half an hour. Since the pain and vertigo continued, they drove to the hospital. Joni transported their four kids to a friend's house and then hurried to the emergency room.

"You've got a concussion," the doctor concluded. After four hours in the emergency room, they sent him home. For the next several days, with everything spinning whenever he moved his head too quickly, Ken stayed in bed as much as possible.

It was a discouraging week for Joni. "Sometimes I have trouble relating because I have always been healthy. As a result, he would get upset with me, and I would feel guilty. It went in a cycle."

Joni does bear extra burdens. Ken says, "I can't tie shoes for kids, change diapers, or pick children up and hold them. When the kids got older, I could sit them, but my main contribution has been to give verbal discipline, moral support, and spiritual support. The actual hands-on, middle-of-the-night, go-help-'em stuff. . . . My wife is such a trooper. She rarely gets the credit she deserves. She's never complained. She just knows that I do what I can. She's been there to do the physical things, both for me and the four kids."

Besides her deep affection and love for Ken, what has helped Joni through the emotional valleys when she doesn't feel like dealing with hardships?

"When I first met Ken," she remembers, "God put in my heart that it didn't matter what a person's handicap was; they should be loved like anyone else. I felt that very strongly. When something happens like that fall and the following week, I have to rely on the Lord and the love that He did give me for Ken and the commitment that I have made. If discouragement gets too big, I go to the Lord and ask Him to help me get things in perspective and not let all the little things tear that away."

She has learned that loyalty is not just a feeling. "Faithfulness is a day-by-day thing," says Joni. "It's a decision you make. I keep going back to our first commitment. It was very clear when Ken and I decided to get married that it was God's will. I go back to the love that has carried us through the years. On bad days if I relied on the feelings of the moment, sometimes I'd run."

Faithfulness in relationships means sticking steadfastly to people despite negatives. A faithful person is loyal to a sick family member, loyal to aging parents, loyal to an unemployed church member, loyal to their spouse whether attractive or not. Selfish concerns—such as convenience, "self-fulfillment," and lust—are not allowed to shear God-ordained bonds.

One demure woman in the Bible teaches us the numerous blessings of such loyalty. She was a pagan. That is, a Gentile, from Moab, a nation bordering Israel. While a teenage girl, her family became acquainted with some expatriate Jews, a man and his wife and two sons who had fled a famine. In due time Ruth married one of the sons.

They didn't live happily ever after. Shortly, Ruth's young husband died, as well as the family's other men, leaving three widows clinging together for survival. Hearing that the famine had ended in Israel, they decided in desperation to move there. At the border, however, concerned over how difficult it would be in Israel for foreign widows, Ruth's mother-in-law, Naomi, advised the daughters to return home.

Pausing on the dry, pebbled path, Ruth replied, "Don't urge me to leave you or turn back from you. Where you go I will go, and where you stay I will stay. Your people will be my people and your God my God. Where you die I will die, and there I will be buried. May the Lord deal with me, be it ever so severely, if anything but death separates you and me" (Ruth 1:16, 17).

Ruth's tenacious loyalty would have royal consequences. After Naomi's homecoming in Bethlehem, Ruth began gleaning barley from a nearby field. The owner, a relative of Naomi's, grew to admire her: "All my fellow townsmen know that you are a woman of noble character," he said. Eventually they married.

Ruth conceived and bore a son, whom they named Obed. Years later Obed became the father of Jesse, and Jesse fathered a ruddy, handsome boy named David. Ruth, the teen-age girl born with neither privilege nor honor nor relationship with God, goes down in history as the great-grandmother of Israel's greatest king.

As did Ruth, we will enjoy five blessings from loyalty:

1. *Loyalty leads us in God's will.* Without faithfulness, Ruth would have languished in Moab. But each act of loyalty—at the time, decisions seemingly more costly than gainful—brought Ruth one step closer to God's perfect will: a husband, children, security, her inspiring story in the Bible, her lineage to the throne. Therefore, at times of uncertainty about God's will, we should ask, what is the faithful thing to do?

2. *Loyalty brings reward.* When Boaz, Ruth's future husband, first saw her gleaning in the fields and learned who she was, he commanded his workers to treat her well. The reason: "I've been told all about what you have done for your mother-in-law since the death of your husband—how you left your father and mother and homeland and came to live with a people you did not know before. May the Lord repay you for what you have done. May you be richly rewarded by the Lord . . ." (Ruth 2:11, 12). In today's vernacular, faithfulness was the secret of her success.

3. *Loyalty earns favor.* As an alien, Ruth should have had all strikes against her in Israel. Nevertheless, everyone in Beth-

lehem respected her. At Obed's birth they said to Naomi, "Ruth loves you and is better to you than seven sons."

4. *Loyalty inspires loyalty in return.* Boaz, although a relative, didn't appear to have been actively supporting the two widows, until he saw Ruth's loyalty first towards Naomi, then himself.

5. *Loyalty triggers a chain reaction of blessings for many people.* Ruth's faithfulness first enriched Naomi, then Boaz, then all the townspeople who were inspired by her character, then all Israel through her heir, King David, and finally all mankind through the Son of David—Jesus Christ.

Words

June 8, 1989. Surely this would be a safe promise. After one inning in Philadelphia, the Pittsburgh Pirates led the Phillies 10-0. The Pirates' radio announcer, Jim Rooker, commented, "If we don't win this one, I don't think I'd want to be on that plane ride home. As a matter of fact, if we don't win, I'll *walk* back to Pittsburgh."

The final score: Philadelphia 15, the Pirates 11. Sure his promise was good old-fashioned baseball hyperbole, but Rooker took it seriously. Four months later, the baseball season over, he began walking. After twelve days and 315 miles, he finally marched into Pittsburgh's Three Rivers Stadium, much the worse for wear. "From the ankles down," he said, "I feel like I've been stabbed with ice picks." Nevertheless, somewhat belatedly, he had kept his word.

That makes him an exceptional person. While anyone can stand behind words that cost nothing, only a faithful man "keeps his oath even when it hurts . . ." (Psalm 15:4). As this verse implies, there is a price tag on our bona fide words, in time, money, work, and the loss of freedom or convenience, which explains the rarity of trustworthiness.

For some people, their word is their bond, for others a blackout. With the latter, words are a smoke screen, an image-keeping facade, mere checkers on a board, oily tools for manipulation. Usefulness expended, they are abandoned. But for the faithful person, words serve as a contract, an accurate signal of intention, an obligation to be fulfilled whether convenient, expedient, or profitable. Such trustworthiness demands great perseverance.

Several years ago I performed a wedding ceremony for a couple who did not attend our church. Afterward the groom handed me an envelope containing a surprisingly generous check for a hundred dollars. It was an answer to prayer, since we were battling some bills, and I deposited it immediately.

Two weeks later I was again surprised: A letter from my bank returned the check stamped "nonsufficient funds." I got a sick feeling. Hoping the groom had overlooked something, I redeposited it. The check rebounded into my mailbox. So I waited a month and tried again . . . and again, "nonsufficient funds." Finally I accepted my loss.

I've also accepted, and no doubt given, some NSF promises in my day. They are just as disheartening.

Thus, trustworthy words are the sound currency of all relationships. As experienced businessmen know, even a written contract is virtually worthless without integrity. With the proliferation of counterfeit words, everything disintegrates, from family to government. This explains the poisonous labels for those who play fast and loose with words: two-faced, forked tongue, rat, snake, double-crosser, double-dealer, false friend, phony, fake, shark, come-on man, liar, hypocrite.

It also explains the greatness of others. A young Israeli was riding his donkey to Jerusalem. He traveled quietly, his crippled legs dangling on each side, his face somber, for he knew that, in all likelihood, he was clip-clopping toward death.

For years he had been lying low. Though royal blood coursed in his veins, it was the has-been blood of the previous king, and the grisly protocol of new-dynasty kings called for a slaughter of the former king's heirs lest they revolt. Inevitably, as he had feared, the summons had come.

He arrived in the familiar capital. Hours later, trembling, he entered the presence of the dread king, bowed to the ground, and awaited his fate.

Long before, the king had made up his mind. "Don't be afraid," he said, "for I will surely show you kindness for the sake of your father. . . . I will restore to you all the land that belonged to your grandfather . . . and you will always eat at my table" (2 Samuel 9:7).

The new dinner guest's grandfather was King Saul, his father, Jonathan, his new king, mercifully, David. His name was Mephibosheth (let's call him "Bo" for short). But why did David take such a security risk? Anyone loyal to Saul and bent on rebellion might rally around Bo. Moreover, if so inclined, Bo would be strategically positioned within the corridors of power to forge alliances and undermine David's advisors. It just didn't make sense.

David's curious decision was rooted in the past. After killing Goliath, David befriended Jonathan, Bo's father. They enacted a goodwill covenant, which over the coming months endured even the insane jealousy and assassination attempts of King Saul. Finally, just before David fled for good,

Jonathan (convinced that David would eventually be king) made this request: "Show me unfailing kindness like that of the Lord as long as I live, so that I may not be killed, and do not ever cut off your kindness from my family—not even when the Lord has cut off every one of David's enemies from the face of the earth" (1 Samuel 20: 14, 15). David gladly agreed, and they reaffirmed their oath of friendship. They never saw each other again.

Although the sword of war later consumed both Jonathan and Saul, David never forgot their pact. Bo was the beneficiary. This story reveals four things about how a faithful person stands behind words:

1. *A faithful man sticks to his word without coercion.* Neither a judge nor a contract was forcing David to patronize Bo. Not only was no one reminding him of his promise, no one even knew. If an expedient man, David could have conveniently lapsed into selective amnesia. At his own initiative, he chose total recall. Promises are a matter of principle, not punishment.

2. *A faithful man sticks to his words even if he doesn't profit personally.* David, more than likely never having met Bo, wasn't nostalgically rekindling an old relationship. Neither would Bo bring to the throne room expertise or wealth for David to exploit. Promises are not pursued merely for profit.

3. *A faithful man sticks to his word even at significant cost.* David knew the tab for keeping his promise would be steep. He was pledging to feed and house Mephibosheth for life! Moreover, as already mentioned, he was risking much politically. As far as possible, promises are not undermined by price.

4. *A faithful man sticks to his word even after a long period of time.* Ten to twelve years or more had passed since David had covenanted with Jonathan. Time does not vitiate a vow.

Responsibilities

In 1974 an amazing man marched out of the Philippine jungles. Hiroo Onoda was a Japanese soldier during World War II. A few months prior to Japan's surrender, he had received specific orders: Gather intelligence on enemy movements, sabotage and harass the enemy rear, and "continue carrying out your mission even after the Japanese army surrenders, no matter what happens."

He obeyed to the hilt. For twenty-nine years he survived in the jungle. Finally a Japanese adventurer found him, then brought his former commanding officer to the Philippines with new orders—surrender.

Onoda had devoted his adult life to one thing: his perceived responsibility. Although we can readily criticize him for fanaticism and uncritical obedience to orders, we can, nevertheless, appreciate how seriously he took his obligations. For him, a man's duty was supreme.

Each of us shoulders legitimate responsibilities far more important than Onoda's misguided orders. The work for which we are paid, marriage vows, spiritual gifts, children, aged parents, positions of leadership or teaching in a church, bills—all are embraced tenaciously by the faithful. Faithful people are unselfishly dependable, persevering at their duties despite boredom, other interests, alluring diversions, or fatigue. Although neglecting our obligations would seem easier, in reality we would hurt both ourselves and others.

Few have honed a more razor-sharp sense of responsibility than the Apostle Paul: "Men ought to regard us as servants of Christ. . . . those who have been given a trust must prove faithful. . . . It is the Lord who judges me. . . . At that time each will receive his praise from God" (1 Corinthians 4:1–5). Four critical insights from these verses will strengthen our dependability:

1. *God gives responsibilities*. Everything is the Lord's, not ours to squander or neglect at will. We are managers, not owners, with a moral obligation to care properly for what God entrusts.

2. *We will answer to God for our responsibilities*. Because we are simply managing someone else's "property," we will someday give account, facing the Owner to explain our actions and the results.

3. *Faithfulness is the chief virtue of servants*. Although we may lack extraordinary talent, broad influence, or "success," anyone can faithfully discharge their duties. It is striking that in the Parable of the Talents in Matthew 25:14–30, the neglectful servant was not the man delegated ten talents, but he with only one. Those with fewer responsibilities are sorely tempted to overlook or even despise them—perhaps out of self-pity, low self-image, doubt, or negativism—and thus prove unfaithful. God calls for dependability no matter what the scope of our duties.

4. *Faithfulness brings honor and reward*. This isn't all grim duty. Although it's hard to persevere in responsibilities, it will be more than worth it, for an owner delights in a faithful

manager. God's rewards will so exceed the hardship, self-denial, and discipline that we will wish we had had weightier duties to discharge.

They were jealous. The Israelites saw that they lacked what other nations had: a king. So some leaders traveled to Ramah and sat down with Samuel, their prophet and judge. "You are old," they said, "and your sons do not walk in your ways; now appoint a king to lead us, such as all the other nations have" (1 Samuel 8:5).

Samuel listened sadly to their request, for two reasons: He recognized the spiritual danger (the people would trust in their king rather than God), and he felt personally rejected. Before answering the elders, he prayed for guidance. "Listen to them," said the Lord, "but warn them solemnly."

How would Samuel now respond? Would he go off in a pout, "This is the thanks I get for serving these people all my life!" Would he shirk his responsibilities as spiritual leader of the nation?

His farewell speech would tell the story. Samuel stood before the people, warned against further disobedience, and then outlined his future role in the nation: "As for me, far be it from me that I should sin against the Lord by failing to pray for you. And I will teach you the way that is good and right" (1 Samuel 12:23).

Samuel was no slacker. Accurately perceiving that it would be a sin against God to quit, he resolved to persevere in his duties to the end, despite rejection by the people, old age, and apparent failure (his sons were immoral, and his sheep had strayed from the Lord). A faithful person can do nothing less.

Such people are rare and special indeed. Perseverance

makes them so. Sticking faithfully to others, to their words, and to their responsibilities, they enjoy great favor with both God and men. Their future is something to look forward to: "A faithful man," says Proverbs 28:20, "will be richly blessed." Perseverance—perhaps the greatest daily challenge anyone faces—isn't so boring after all.

12
Resources for Perseverance— Part I

Other racers call him Ironhead. Although in second place by mere inches after the first 160 laps of the 1986 Daytona 500, Dale Earnhardt just completed a disastrous pit stop, taking 19.6 seconds, 4.4 seconds more than the leader, Geoff Bodine. With forty laps to go at better than 200 miles per hour, the gap that had been inches was now a quarter mile.

Ironhead went on the hunt. Tucking up close behind a friend, he rode his draft for 14 laps. Bodine, though leading, was having problems with his tires. Then with only 24 laps left, Ironhead positioned himself right where every Daytona driver dreams to be: snuggled in back of the frontrunner, poised to aerodynamically slingshot out of the final turn into the lead and over the finish line.

Aware of his disadvantage, Bodine actually tried slowing down to squeeze Earnhardt off his tail, but couldn't shake him. Bodine was a goner, everyone knew. With 3 laps remaining, however, two minutes from the checkered flag, Ironhead suddenly faded and drifted into the pits. On lap 197 he had run out of gas.

Desire and determination alone don't propel anyone to the finish line; racers need fuel. Likewise, being convinced of the reasons to persevere is one thing; actually doing it is quite another. We need resources. Thankfully, God has ample supply.

The next two chapters are a perseverance workbook devoted to, first, understanding the fuel resources available to believers and, second, applying them to our daily lives.

I have divided these resources into five categories to show their helpfulness in overcoming five distinctive challenges of perseverance:

1. The challenge of endurance
2. The challenge of persistence
3. The challenge of hopeful waiting on God
4. The challenge of patience
5. The challenge of steadfastness

As we will now see, God has fueled us for triumph in every challenge.

The Challenge of Endurance

Endurance is the strength to continue despite pain, the opposite being weakness and faintheartedness.

Endurance typifies the marathon runner or iron-man competitor. Although the average jogger depletes strength or willpower after so many miles—his carbohydrates exhausted and poisons building up in the muscles—somehow a marathoner keeps tapping deeper reservoirs of energy.

An overcoming Christian life requires equal stamina. Scripture warns that we will face fatigue: "Let us not become weary in doing good . . ." (Galatians 6:9). As well as pain: "It has been granted to you on behalf of Christ not only to believe on him, but also to suffer for him" (Philippians 1:29). As well as hills to climb: "Consider it pure joy, my brothers, whenever you face trials of many kinds" (James 1:2). Yet the Bible also promises that the resources are available for everyone to endure like an iron man.

Endurance Resource #1

God's strength. Even the mightiest humans are desperately weak. One may be relatively stronger than another, but we all have limitations. At that point where weakness, pain, faintheartedness, or fatigue feels overwhelming, a Christian can be "strengthened with all power according to his glorious might," promises Colossians 1:11 "so that you may have great endurance. . . ." Actually, God wants us to rely on His strength not just when we are depleted, but always. "I can do everything through him who gives me strength," says Philippians 4:13.

Teri Chodor recalls times "when I felt so weak. Sometimes I felt, 'I'm so weak, and I'm losing faith so much, she's going to die.' Then I realized it wasn't really depending on me and my strength. It was all God's strength. Even in my weakness, God was still strong. It was a relief for me. For this specific incident, God gave me the strength and the faith."

> Questions: Do I tackle life alone except in emergencies, or do I rely on God's help? Am I proud of my own strength and willpower? Conversely, have I convinced myself I'm weak and, therefore, limited?

165

Solution: Depend continually on the Lord's strength, especially by praying.

Application: Schedule at least five minutes every morning for specific prayer about the day ahead. For each challenge and concern ask for God's strength, help, and wisdom.

Application: Throughout the day as challenges arise, pause for five seconds and silently pray.

Application: At times of despair and weakness, pray, "Lord, strengthen me with the Holy Spirit in my inner person."

Endurance Resource #2

A vital relationship with Jesus. "Come to me, all you who are weary and burdened, and I will give you rest. Take my yoke upon you and learn from me, for I am gentle and humble in heart, and you will find rest for your souls. For my yoke is easy and my burden is light" (Matthew 11:28–30).

These verses describe a happy contradiction. Jesus addresses bone-tired people, those who cannot endure another day, and calls them to shoulder a yoke, the wooden collar worn by oxen while plowing. That hardly sounds restful. Yet the yoke of Christ wears differently, soothingly, bracingly. It is a living relationship with Jesus of love and obedience that restores and refreshes. Even as we plow fields, vital interaction with Jesus renews our strength.

Question: Am I more focused on my problems than on Christ?

Solution: Rekindle your relationship with the Lord by strengthening communication, centering your thoughts more on Him, and obeying His words.

Application: Especially when you feel overwhelmed, take

fifteen minutes and do nothing but worship Jesus, thank Him for His blessings, and express your love. Don't pray about any of your needs until the fifteen minutes are over.

Application: Over the coming weeks read Matthew, Mark, Luke, and John, and list the characteristics of Jesus that impress you. Include those in your thanksgiving and worship.

Application: While reading these gospels, also note the commands of Jesus that you fall especially short of. Firmly decide to follow His direction.

Endurance Resource #3

The example of Christ. Pain hinders endurance. Whether emotional or physical it screams, "Stop what you're doing." Even those with high pain tolerance eventually reach a point where they can hardly bear it any longer. Jesus knows what it's like:

> Let us fix our eyes on Jesus, the author and perfecter of our faith, who for the joy set before him *endured the cross*, scorning its shame, and sat down at the right hand of the throne of God. Consider him who endured such opposition from sinful men, so that you will not grow weary and lose heart.
>
> Hebrews 12:2, 3 (italics added)

According to this Scripture, by meditating on the sufferings of Christ, we find courage to carry our own cross.

Question: Have I lost perspective on my pain and hardship, forgetting the price Jesus paid for me?

Solution: Compare your agony to that of Jesus Christ and seek inspiration in His example.

Application: In the following Scripture portions, list the specific pangs, both physical and otherwise, that our Lord endured: Matthew 26:1—27:61; Isaiah 52:13—53:12.

Application: When suffering, reread these Scriptures.

Solution: Recognize the prevalence of suffering among followers of the Lord.

Application: Study the tribulations of other believers in the following Scriptures: 2 Corinthians 4:7–12; 6:3–10; 11:22–23; Hebrews 11.

The Challenge of Persistence

Persistence is exertion toward a goal no matter the amount of time or attempts required. Persistence stresses activity and determination. The opposite would be passive resignation.

The king of Scotland, Robert Bruce, was hiding in a cave. He had just suffered another crushing defeat by the English, but that was not the immediate focus of his attention. Instead, his eyes were set on an industrious spider. Six times it had scaled the wall only to fall before reaching the roof. "Now shall this spider teach me what I am to do," he said, "for I also have failed six times." Finally on the seventh ascent, it reached the top and spun a web. Encouraged, he ventured from the cave, gathered followers, and defeated the English at Turnberry Castle.

Unfortunately, the story of a never-say-die spider isn't quite enough to inspire most of us to persistence. God has supplied far superior resources.

Persistence Resource #1

The renewal of the inner man. Even when our lives are free from pain, we may be tempted to quit because of boredom, despair, or burnout. Motivation is a problem that God can solve. "Therefore we do not lose heart. Though outwardly we are wasting away, yet inwardly we are being renewed day by day" (2 Corinthians 4:16).

> **Questions: Do I dislike what I'm doing? Do I fulfill my responsibilities more out of obligation than desire? Is my joy gone? Do I dread each day?**

Solution: Renew the inner man by cultivating your devotional walk with God.

Application: Schedule a daily appointment with the Lord. First decide on a regular time and place alone. Then establish a Bible reading plan; that is, how many chapters to cover daily and in what sections of the Bible (for example, two chapters in the New Testament and one in the Old). Consider the plans available in Christian bookstores for reading through the Bible in a year. Third, choose a prayer outline. In his book *The Hour That Changes the World*, Dick Eastman suggests this format: praise, waiting, confession, Scripture praying, watching, intercession, petition, thanksgiving, singing, meditation, listening, praise. Others, such as Larry Lea in *Could You Not Tarry One Hour*, suggest the Lord's Prayer as a framework. Finally, tell a close Christian friend about your plans and request a weekly checkup on your follow-through.

Solution: Attend church religiously.

Application: Schedule a minimum of once each week in

worship services, to be broken only in case of disaster. Make this a solemn commitment to God. Recognize that the reasons for skipping church mustered in the past have been mere excuses and repent before God for neglecting the household of faith. Tell your pastor and another friend of your new commitment.

Persistence Resource #2

A *fuller perspective.* Like trying to build a sand castle near the waves, much of our effort can seem pointless when we focus merely on the here and now. But our work has infinitely greater significance. "For our light and momentary troubles are achieving for us an eternal glory that far outweighs them all. So we fix our eyes not on what is seen, but on what is unseen. For what is seen is temporary, but what is unseen is eternal" (2 Corinthians 4:17, 18). "You know that the Lord will reward everyone for whatever good he does . . ." (Ephesians 6:8).

> **Questions: Am I losing heart because of apparent failure? Do I feel unappreciated? Am I looking primarily for results in this world?**

Solution: Maintain an eternal perspective. Reorder your ultimate priorities, values, and goals around what lasts forever. Remind yourself that ultimate results will never be seen in this world, but in the kingdom of God.

Application: At times of despair, schedule a morning or afternoon alone with God. Spend at least two hours reading the Bible (suggested Scriptures: Psalm 127:1, 2; Psalm 90; Romans 12; Philippians 1—4; Matthew 5—7; Revelation 1—5, 19—22; Matthew 16:13–28; Matthew 24, 25; 1 Corinthians

1; Ecclesiastes 12:13, 14). Before reading ask the Lord to reveal things in your perspective that are earth-bound. Ask Him to open your eyes to an eternal viewpoint on your life. Afterward review your goals, values, priorities, activities, commitments, and responsibilities. Try to see them as God does.

Persistence Resource #3

A *worthy purpose.* Just as immunologists, motivated by compassion for sick people, have been able to continue their vaccine research for years if need be, so the more noble our purpose, the greater our persistence. "Whatever you do, work at it with all your heart, as working for the Lord, not for men. . . . It is the Lord Christ you are serving " (Colossians 3:23, 24).

> Question: Do I do things primarily for the Lord, myself, or others?

Solution: Above all, seek to please the Lord.

Application: When wavering, pause and examine your motivations, asking yourself, "Who am I most trying to please right now? Whose feelings am I most concerned about?" Then rededicate yourself to pleasing the Lord.

Persistence Resource #4

The call of God. God is great, awesome, overwhelming. As sovereign Lord, His words shake heaven and earth. Simply because the Almighty has called and commissioned us, we always have a compelling reason to persist. "Brothers, each man, as responsible to God, should remain in the situation God called him to" (1 Corinthians 7:24).

Vince Chodor, at the outset of their crisis with Rebekah, as he was reeling from the bad news and trying to catch his bearings, found this reason compelling. "The breakthrough for me was to decide on my philosophy of life. The Scripture that helped me was in Ecclesiastes, where Solomon said he had tried all the things we can do in life, and the bottom line is, you have to love and serve God."

> **Questions: What is most important to me, what God wants or what I want? What value do I place on the virtue of simply serving the Lord?**

Solution: Dedicate yourself to wholeheartedly follow the call of God.

Application: As you read the Bible, write down the callings/responsibilities especially relevant for your life. Memorize the most significant Scriptures.

Application: Write down your perception of God's will in the major responsibilities of your life. If unsure, discuss it with your pastor or another mature believer. Hereafter when struggling, remind yourself that you don't do this because you always feel like it, but because you delight in following your heavenly Father. Then pray: "Lord, I recognize Your call on my life, and I rededicate myself to serving You by the power of the Holy Spirit. Thank You for revealing Your good, pleasing, and perfect will."

Persistence Resource #5

The spiritual law of sowing and reaping. We can be encouraged with the knowledge that no effort unto the Lord is wasted. Every deed is a seed remembered and cultivated by God. ". . . A man reaps what he sows. . . . Let us not become weary in doing good, for at the proper time we will reap a harvest if we do not give up" (Galatians 6:7, 9).

Question: Am I discouraged primarily because I see no results from my efforts?

Solution: Put your confidence in the spiritual law of sowing and reaping. Keep sowing seeds until the harvest comes.

Application: As you approach tasks that seem fruitless, say a prayer of dedication: "Lord, I commit this deed to You as a seed in the soil of the kingdom. Please water it and enable me to reap someday."

The Challenge of Hopeful Waiting on God

Hopeful waiting on God is the ongoing confidence that the Lord will someday meet a need. The emphasis is on God's future help and the tenacious hope it inspires. The opposite would be despair or striving efforts to solve a problem without God.

Recently I mailed an important letter to my health insurance company. Enclosed were four months of bills from doctors and dentists for care on my family of six. Starting a week later, with my hopes set on a refund check, I began keenly anticipating the mail, checking the box every hour or two when at home, or by phone, asking my wife, "Anything in the mail today?" Receiving nothing, I would be momentarily disappointed, but then rebound and start hoping in tomorrow and imminent financial relief. After a month of that, the check arrived—and it was larger than I had anticipated. In like manner, God wants us to wait in hope for His help.

The psalmist put it this way:

I wait for the Lord, my soul waits, and in his word I put my hope. My soul waits for the Lord more than watchmen wait for the morning, more than watchmen wait for the morning. O Israel, put your hope in the Lord, for with the Lord is unfailing love and with him is full redemption.

Psalm 130:5–7

Hopeful Waiting Resource #1

God's promises of help, salvation, and deliverance. Those who hope in God are not just positive thinkers, Pollyannas, dreamers. We have an objective reason for our hope. "For I am the Lord, your God, who takes hold of your right hand and says to you, Do not fear; I will help you" (Isaiah 41:13).

Our open access to the Lord in prayer. "Call to me and I will answer you . . ." (Jeremiah 33:3).

Questions: In the face of troubles, do I view God as someone who wants to actively work on my behalf? Am I trying to solve my problems without Him?

Solution: Trust in God's promises of personal help and salvation for all daily needs. Pray accordingly.

Application: Make prayer the first step of any problem-solving plan.

Application: The next time you face a major difficulty, schedule thirty minutes once a week for prayer about each detail of the problem.

Application: Memorize Proverbs 3:5, 6. Quote and meditate on it at times of anxiety.

Hopeful Waiting Resource #2

Insight into the means to lasting results. It is easier to resist carnal striving and wait for God if we know what our unaided efforts would produce. "Unless the Lord builds the house, its builders labor in vain . . ." (Psalm 127:1). Only what God does through us will count for eternity.

Tony and Barb recall that "our tendency was to figure out a man-made way to get rid of our financial problems. But our only successes came when we stood on God's Word. If we were being disobedient about something, our breakthrough would not come. We could do anything we wanted. We could make rounds, we could do this and that. We tried all of it. The breakthrough would not come until we did what God wanted us to do spiritually. It wasn't anything man-made."

Question: Is my ultimate hope in myself, hard work, others, the world, or is it in the Lord?

Solution: Recognize that all human efforts apart from Christ eventually crumble to dust. Let God build your life.

Application: Record for one week how much time you spend seeking the Lord in Bible reading, prayer, and church involvement. Do the numbers suggest solid reliance on the Lord? Ask Him for wisdom concerning adjustments.

Application: Total last year's financial giving to Christian ministry. What percentage is it of gross earnings? Does it indicate strong reliance on the Lord as your ultimate source for all things?

Hopeful Waiting Resource #3

The Scriptures. Daily troubles wage a war of attrition against our hope. Well aware of this, God has supplied a means for daily reinforcement. "Through endurance and the encouragement of the Scriptures we might have hope" (Romans 15:4).

> **Questions: When struggling with despair, do my thoughts turn to God's truth, or do I worry? Am I giving God a chance to inspire hope?**

Solution: Read the Bible daily.

Application: When disheartened, read the Bible until you find a relevant promise, then memorize it. Quote it three times every hour until it sinks into your heart and repeat it every time depression threatens.

Hopeful Waiting Resource #4

Our spiritual inheritance. ". . . Those who hope in the Lord will inherit the land" (Psalm 37:9). "An inheritance quickly gained at the beginning will not be blessed at the end" (Proverbs 20:21). Most of us want God's highest purpose and blessing. This is symbolized in the Bible by the idea of inheritance. God prepares an inheritance—a good destiny—for each of His children, but it must not be grabbed prematurely. Like the prodigal son who hastily gobbled up his share of his father's inheritance, then squandered it in a foreign land, we often try to rush God into bestowing our future. However, only He knows when we are ready to receive, whether soon or late. He is preparing us to be able to retain His maximum blessing.

> **Questions: Do I believe that God has a high purpose for me? In the past, have I intended to get what I want out of life whether the Lord grants it or not?**

Solution: Establish in your mind that the key to inheriting God's highest call and blessing is to hope in Him and wait for Him.

Application: Make it a personal policy that whenever you feel like doing something hasty, you transfer that energy into thirty minutes of seeking the Lord. Pipe haste-energy into prayer-energy.

When Dale Earnhardt ran out of gas at Daytona, it really wasn't an oversight. He had taken a calculated risk. Although low on fuel, he knew that if he took a pit stop he would lose his position; if he continued, he might be able to finish the race. Fortunately, we don't face that decision. In fact, unlike racing, we win by making as many pit stops as possible.

13
Resources for Perseverance— Part II

One year after his 1986 Daytona 500 victory over the gas-depleted Dale Earnhardt, Geoff Bodine once again was leading the 1987 Daytona by a full mile with 4 laps remaining. But on lap 197, in a carbon copy of Ironhead's fade of the year before, this time Bodine ran dry. He, too, had taken a measured risk: Thirty laps earlier, when trailing the others, he had intentionally skipped taking a pit stop with the leaders, estimating it was his only chance to beat the powerhouse front-runner, Bill Elliott.

There is always a price for refueling, but it is one that finishers pay. God's resources are received through effort, intentional application, and diligence. Too many believers try to casually run on fumes and as a result fade before the check-ered flag.

We have explored resources for three of the five challenges of perseverance. In this chapter we will see how to top off the tank for the final two: patience and steadfastness.

The Challenge of Patience

Patience is the attitude of submission to God that enables us to contentedly continue in His will. It emphasizes attitude more than activity. The opposite would be paroxysms of anger or frustration as well as impulsiveness.

For example, the more an athlete trusts his coach, the more patiently he will train. I remember when I was a college freshman, and my gymnastics coach held me back, instructing me to delete some difficult moves from my routines. He felt that in a year or two, with greater strength and ability, I would be able to perform the difficult skills more consistently. Although my pride preferred flashier tricks, I patiently went along, believing he knew what was best. In the same way, confidence in the Lord and His purposes enables us to obey His speed limits.

Patience Resource #1

The infilling of God's Spirit. Emotions are powerful, sometimes seemingly irresistible, but they are not stronger than God's presence within us. "The fruit of the Spirit is love, joy, peace, *patience*, kindness, goodness, faithfulness, gentleness and self-control . . ." (Galatians 5:22, 23 italics added).

Question: Do I lack the sense that God is in my heart helping me deal with my emotions, thoughts, and decisions?

Solution: Seek the continual infilling of the Holy Spirit.
Application: Regularly pray, "Lord, fill me more and more with Your Holy Spirit. Reveal any sins that are grieving or inhibiting the Spirit in me."

Application: Using a Bible concordance, look up every reference to the Spirit of God in the New Testament. (This will take several periods of study.) Write down anything the verses teach about how to experience a deeper anointing of the Spirit. Put these lessons into practice.

Patience Resource #2

Contentment in Christ. No one can be patient while their deepest desires are stymied. But when we long most for Christ Himself, contentment is always possible. "For to me, to live is Christ . . ." said Paul in Philippians 1:21. Later he continued, "I know what it is to be in need, and I know what it is to have plenty. I have learned the secret of being content in any and every situation, whether well fed or hungry, whether living in plenty or in want. I can do everything through him who gives me strength" (Philippians 4:12, 13).

One experienced Christian recently said to me, "This is real life. It isn't pretty all the time, and it doesn't have easy answers. But one thing I've learned, even with those difficult things you've gotta go through, Christ is the only way."

Question: Am I discontent with my life, feeling I can't be happy without more things, accomplishments, friends, or experiences?

Solution: Center your ambitions and desires in Jesus Christ. Make Him the axis of everything, your first love.

Application: Read the Gospel of John and note the names and characteristics given for Christ (such as "bread of life," "living water," "Son of God"). Make these the content of daily worship.

Application: In prayer, learn to celebrate who Jesus is and what He has done, much like a sports fan would celebrate a team championship.

Patience Resource #3

The catharsis of prayer. What can we do with bottled up anxieties and frustrations? In 1 Samuel 1:15, Hannah describes her prayer as "pouring out my soul to the Lord." God is always there, always attentive and concerned. Pouring out our thoughts and emotions to the Wonderful Counselor far surpasses getting things off our chest with others. "Cast all your anxiety on him," says 1 Peter 5:7, "because he cares for you."

For instance, when they first learned of their daughter's heart troubles, Teri remembers, "We fell on our faces before the Lord. I hardly knew how to pray. All I could say was, 'Jesus, help!' "

Supernatural peace resulting from prayer. "Do not be anxious about anything, but in everything, by prayer and petition, with thanksgiving, present your requests to God. And the peace of God, which transcends all understanding, will guard your hearts and your minds in Christ Jesus" (Philippians 4:6, 7). Supernatural peace enables supernatural patience.

After those times of prayer, Teri remembers, "The peace was supernatural. God was just putting it into me."

Questions: Do I regularly reach the point where my feelings are unbearable? Do I tend to do harmful things when upset?

Solution: In times of distress, get alone with God and completely unburden your heart to Him.

Application: What is your reflex at times of emotional upheaval? Most have an escape valve, whether something harmful like alcohol or drugs, or something good like calling a friend. Let your first reflex be soul-outpouring prayer for at least thirty minutes. Use the thought of your old-habit reflex as a trigger for prayer.

Application: Specifically ask the Lord for His peace.

Patience Resource #4

Devotion to God's will. Sometimes we may feel that our lot in life is all bad, that a day is something to get over with. Despite that perception, even in the most terrible situations we can always do "God's . . . good, pleasing and perfect will" (Romans 12:2). His meaningful will is available even in torment ("Love your enemies," for example). Since God does not reserve the good life merely for the future, but avails it now in His good, pleasing, and perfect will, patience is always possible.

> Question: Am I often upset because my life agenda is frustrated?

Solution: Not only submit yourself to the will of God, but seek it as your highest goal in every circumstance. Believe that it excels your own will.

Application: Memorize Romans 12:2. At difficult times quote and meditate on it.

Patience Resource #5

Our cross. When we strain with impatience, the sinful nature within, surging with pride, self, and passions, is usually no small culprit. If we are willing, however, the sinful nature can be handcuffed. "If anyone would come after me, he must deny himself and take up his cross daily and follow me. For whoever wants to save his life will lose it, but whoever loses his life for me will save it. What good is it for a man to gain the whole world, and yet lose or forfeit his very self?" (Luke 9:23–25).

Question: Am I totally committed to Christ rather than self?

Solution: Deny sinful desires. Die to self and live for Christ.

Application: At times of emotional distress ask yourself these questions: What are my motivations? Could they be such things as selfishness, pride, envy, or covetousness? If so, confess to the Lord, then request forgiveness and cleansing. Consciously choose to die to that sinful desire, in other words, to say no, to deny that impulse any influence over your thoughts or will.

Patience Resource #6

God's comfort. While suffering pain, whether physical or emotional, we find it especially difficult to calmly wait. But God knows something about relief. "Praise be to the God and Father of our Lord Jesus Christ, the Father of compassion and the God of all comfort, who comforts us in all our troubles. . . . For just as the sufferings of Christ flow over into our lives, so also through Christ our comfort overflows" (2 Corinthians 1:3–5).

Question: Is my pain wrenching me off the tracks of God's will?

Solution: Seek the analgesic comfort available in the things of God.

Application: Schedule intensive-care treatment. For two weeks, double your usual time of Bible reading, prayer, and church attendance/fellowship.

Application: Meanwhile, specifically ask God to comfort you daily.

The Challenge of Steadfastness

Steadfastness is the ability to stand firm despite adversity. The opposite would be a wavering, erratic double-mindedness.

King David commanded some steadfast followers. One of his warriors, a member of the elite squadron called David's Mighty Men, showed his mettle in a skirmish with the Philistines. When the rest of the troops retreated, "he stood his ground and struck down the Philistines till his hand grew tired and froze to the sword" (2 Samuel 23:10). One man, standing immovable with God's help, against an entire army. And he prevailed. "The Lord brought about a great victory that day. . . ."

Just as surely, the Lord bolsters us to stand our ground.

Steadfastness Resource #1

Our relationship with an unchanging God. No one can find firm footing on the sand of this unstable world. But "Jesus Christ is the same yesterday and today and forever" (Hebrews 13:8). ". . . And he will stand, for the Lord is able to make him stand" (Romans 14:4).

Question: Am I trying to establish my life on the Lord, or on money, career, a network of friends, personal strength?

Solution: Build your foundation on the Lord. Be conscious of God and acknowledge Him throughout the day.

Application: Whenever we exclude God our Rock, we invite instability. Therefore, examine your life for any areas currently off-limits to the Lord, such as finances, sexual conduct, thought patterns, speech, goals, marriage, or education, and thoroughly relinquish control.

Application: Develop a greater awareness of the Lord by voicing one-sentence prayers of thanksgiving, praise, and request throughout the day. Do so at least once per hour.

Steadfastness Resource #2

Faith in God. ". . . It is by faith you stand firm" (2 Corinthians 1:24). ". . . If you do not stand firm in your faith, you will not stand at all" (Isaiah 7:9). The cure for double-mindedness, which is the primary cause of instability, is the single-mindedness of faith. God only stabilizes us to the extent that we believe.

Through all his financial trials as a photographer, Tony knows "my faith in God has sustained me in this business. I tell people that if it wasn't for my faith in God, I never could have stuck it out."

Question: When troubles arise, do I waver with doubt?

Solution: Maintain faith in the Lord even in the worst peril.
Application: Read Hebrews 11 every day for a week.

Record anything you learn about the meaning of faith. As the chapter refers to different individuals from the Bible and their stories, compare your circumstances to theirs and imitate how they believed in God.

Application: Using a concordance, read every verse with the word *faith* in the four Gospels. Memorize those that speak most forcefully to you.

Application: Read the story of Abraham, who is the greatest model of faith in the Bible, in Genesis 12—25. Note any parallels between his life and yours. Imitate his faith.

Steadfastness Resource #3

God's Word. "All men are like grass, and all their glory is like the flowers of the field; the grass withers and the flowers fall, but the word of the Lord stands forever" (1 Peter 1:24, 25). In the struggle to stand fast, our mind is the pivot point, the battleground, the axis. God's firm truth thus provides a necessary cornerstone.

Teri Chodor recalls the effect of God's Word in her mind at the times when doctors would list dangers ahead for Rebekah: "Even when the doctor would be giving me bad news, I would hear Scriptures in my head, counteracting what he was saying, though not denying it, accepting what he was saying but knowing that God could change it."

> **Questions: Do I take my life-style cues from TV shows, the newspaper, and magazines, or from the Bible? Do I consult the Bible and godly counsel when I face moral/ethical decisions?**

Solution: Respect and believe the Bible as final and infallible truth for daily life. Resolve to learn the Scriptures.

Application: Become a lifelong Bible student. Plan not only daily reading, but also periodic study. Set a weekly appointment of one hour for intensive Bible research. At a Bible bookstore, purchase a book on how to study the Bible, as well as the basic study tools needed, such as a concordance and a Bible dictionary/encyclopedia.

Steadfastness Resource #4

Spiritual armor. Certainly another cause of instability is the militant opposition of Satan. But God has fully armed us for defense.

> Therefore put on the full armor of God, so that when the day of evil comes, you may be able to stand your ground, and after you have done everything, to stand. Stand firm then, with the belt of truth buckled around your waist, with the breastplate of righteousness in place, and with your feet fitted with the readiness that comes from the gospel of peace. In addition to all this, take up the shield of faith, with which you can extinguish all the flaming arrows of the evil one. Take the helmet of salvation and the sword of the Spirit, which is the word of God. And pray in the Spirit on all occasions. . . .
>
> Ephesians 6:13–18

Teri Chodor remembers the conflict: "The devil puts horrible thoughts in your mind and heart, and if you don't have anything to fight that with, you are overcome by fear."

Questions: When it seems I am under spiritual blitzkrieg, do I usually end up the loser? Do I feel defenseless?

Solution: Put on the whole armor of God. Leave no vulnerabilities.

Application: Read Ephesians 6:10–19 and list each piece of armor, first naming the metaphor and then the spiritual counterpart. Determine how well you are currently employing them. Correct weaknesses.

Steadfastness Resource #5

Prayer partners. Even when we cannot muster the wherewithal to stand firm, the intercession of others can sustain us. "Epaphras . . . is always wrestling in prayer for you, that you may stand firm in all the will of God, mature and fully assured" (Colossians 4:12).

Questions: Do I feel alone in this struggle? Do I feel unable to pray effectively for myself?

Solution: At times of weakness, request prayer from others.

Application: Call three believers who intercede regularly and request prayer for a specific time period, such as seven days. As a reminder and guideline, mail each a letter that briefly and specifically describes your need. Later, inform them of any progress resulting from their prayers.

Steadfastness Resource #6

God's command. "Therefore, my dear brothers, stand firm. Let nothing move you . . ." (1 Corinthians 15:58). On the battlefield, when hearts begin to melt under adversity, sending a wave of panic over the soldiers, the sergeant's iron command, "Stand firm, hold your positions," can in itself galvanize willpower.

Questions: When I make important, life-directing decisions, do I base them mainly on my feelings? Do I rationalize inconstancy, saying that it's just my personality, that I'm weak or have problems others don't?

Solution: Focus less on your feelings and more on God's commands. Resolve to obey the Lord, remembering that right feelings eventually follow right actions.

Solution: Recognize that God's will is steadfastness. Never rationalize wishy-washiness.

Application: Memorize 1 Corinthians 15:58. At times of double-mindedness, quote it and declare aloud, "I'm going to obey the Lord by standing firm."

*   *   *

"It hit me all at once at Rebekah's first birthday party," says Vince. "I remember looking at her and for the first time realizing that it *was* all over. All the negative stuff, all the blood, all the tubes, were behind us now. I remember thinking, *God, how could anybody doubt You after what I'm looking at, a baby smiling and laughing, and all the relatives finally being happy after what everyone had gone through, how many previous times we were all together but in tears and sorrow.*"

The party was a celebration indeed. One hundred euphoric people—family, friends, church members, neighbors—crowded into Vince and Teri's side yard on a cloudless, eighty-degree July day. Christian music played through the window, a clown entertained, the kids broke open a heart-shaped piñata. A poster by the refreshments displayed photos of Rebekah in the hospital, EKGs, and other medical reports, and the key Scripture promises that had carried them through the crisis.

The triumphant note was in the refrigerator. Toward the end of the day, Vince pulled out the cake, heaped with whipped cream and decorated with a pink heart, which said, "My flesh and my heart may fail, but God is the strength of my heart." In the center stood a lone candle, one that few had thought would ever be lit.

Minutes later, after everyone had sung "Happy Birthday," Teri leaned over and blew out the candle for her daughter, then said, "Praise the Lord, Rebekah!" As usual, Rebekah lifted her tiny arms in the air, then stuck her hand in the cake.

The emotion and message of this day had begun hours earlier. One of their relatives, a man who generally keeps his feelings to himself, was delivering folding chairs for the party. When he pulled up in front of the house, he immediately noticed something different: a thirty-foot banner tied to the front fence with a five-word message printed in huge capital letters. For several minutes he sat alone in the car, overcome with emotion.

When he started moving the chairs into the house, Teri asked, "Do you want something to drink?"

Keeping conveniently busy, "Uh, uh," was all he could reply, and then he left without a word, later returning to his own home still overwhelmed. The five simple words on the banner

that had triggered such uncharacteristic emotion: "BE
HE LIVES, SHE LIVES."

Because He lives, actively involved in our present a
future, all of us, in the face of even the fiercest hardship
go on, and on, and on, to the very finish of the mid
marathon.

that had triggered such uncharacteristic emotion: "BECAUSE HE LIVES, SHE LIVES."

Because He lives, actively involved in our present and our future, all of us, in the face of even the fiercest hardships, can go on, and on, and on, to the very finish of the midnight marathon.